THERE'S A METHOD TO THE MADNESS

THERE'S A
METHOD
TO THE
MADNESS

Building Blocks For A Small Business

Nichcol Collins

Xulon Elite

Xulon Press Elite
555 Winderley Pl, Suite 225
Maitland, FL 32751
407.339.4217
www.xulonpress.com

© 2024 by Nichcol Collins

The author has made every effort to provide accurate information regarding the subject matter in this book. Any inaccuracies or errors are not intentional. Any similarities found between this book and other forms of work are purely coincidental.

This book is published for educational purposes only. The author makes no promises that any advice listed in the book will lead to guaranteed results. Readers are advised to use any information, opinion, or advice obtained from this book at their own discretion and risk.

Any business decisions should not be made before consulting a professional advisor, doing your own research, and due diligence. The author disclaims any liability in case any information, advice, opinion, or recommendation in this book ends up being inaccurate, unreliable, or incomplete or does not yield expected results for the readers. The author has neither liability nor responsibility to any person or entity in case of any damage or loss caused either directly or indirectly by this book.

All rights reserved solely by the author. The author guarantees all contents are original and do not infringe upon the legal rights of any other person or work. No part of this book may be reproduced in any form without the permission of the author.

Due to the changing nature of the Internet, if there are any web addresses, links, or URLs included in this manuscript, these may have been altered and may no longer be accessible. The views and opinions shared in this book belong solely to the author and do not necessarily reflect those of the publisher. The publisher therefore disclaims responsibility for the views or opinions expressed within the work.

Paperback ISBN-13: 978-1-66289-992-8
Ebook ISBN-13: 978-1-66289-993-5

Table of Contents

Preface ix
Chapter 1 – Yes, There is Homework 1
    Why do you want to become an entrepreneur?
    The Need for Market Research
    How to Conduct Market Research
Chapter 2: Define the Target 13
    Buyer Persona
    Using Your Research to Create Buyer Personas
    Value Proposition
Chapter 3: The Purpose of It All 29
    Vision Statement
    Mission Statement
    Cultural Statement
Chapter 4: Brand Matters 33
    Why does it matter?
    Finding the Perfect Brand Name
    Don'ts of Naming Your Business
    Building your Brand
Chapter 5: The Legal Stuff 51
    Establish a Legal Business Structure
    Register Your Works
    Taxes Your Business Must Pay

    Business Insurance
    Purchasing the Best Insurance for Your Small Business
Chapter 6: The Money 71
    Determine Financial Needs
    Create a Budget
    Establish a Business Accounting System
    Establish a Business Bank Account
    You Need a D-U-N-S
    Get a Business Line of Credit
    Secured and Unsecured Business Credit Card
    Payment Gateway Selection
Chapter 7: Team Worthy 85
    What to Look for When You're Hiring
    Red Flags to Watch out for in Candidates
    Keeping a Winning Team
Chapter 8: Brand Marketing 93
    Marketing You
    Increase Sales with Marketing Materials
    Sociably Winning
    Substance Strong
    Reputation Excellence
    Direct Style
    Ads
Chapter 9: Revenue, Business Model & Business Plan 101
    Revenue Model
    Business Model
    Business Plan

Chapter 10: Embracing Failure 117
    Types of Failure
    Recovering From Failure
    Getting Back on Track
    Author Bio
    Works Cited

Preface

If you've been slaving away at your corporate job and feel like you've had your fair share of working for someone else's business, then it's time for you to take a step back and evaluate your options.

Do you have something of service that you can offer to the world?
A business idea that will take the market by storm executed correctly!
Maybe being your own boss is the big adventure you've been looking for.

When you're in charge of a business, it seems like life couldn't get any better. You set your own hours, work for yourself, and the best part of all – there's no one else but you to answer to. But in all honesty, this couldn't be further from the truth. Ask anyone who's built a business from scratch. They have had their work cut out for them, and it can take months, even years, to get to a place of comfort.

Transitioning from being employed to becoming an entrepreneur is not an easy road to take. When you're the one making all the decisions, you are also held responsible for any problems or failures.

You have two options: either copy the business plans of other successful businesses or create your own unique plan. But guess what? The perfect business plan doesn't exist. Somebody else's recipe for success might not yield the same results for your business. You must develop unique strategies to succeed in a competitive market.

Successful entrepreneurs know when to test their hypotheses and when to implement their plans. They may not get everything right in the beginning, but it's their willingness to keep going back to the basics and rethink their business strategies in the face of adversity that truly helps their business grow against all odds.

Starting a small business is a process riddled with challenges and failures (**Articles - Investopedia, 2021**) right from the get-go, but if you're game to learn and you prioritize your consumer's needs before anything else, then you're on the right track. Remember, success may not be a constant, but your hard work should be. When you put in the hours, learn from your mistakes, and listen to your customers every step of the way, you can expect the highest returns.

The thing about starting your own business is that it's a lot like putting a puzzle together, you start with the outside (your foundation) and then you fill in the inside (your consumer's, etc.) Steve Jobs became successful because he knew how to put the right pieces together, not because he knew everything. It's important to know when to do the work and when to outsource it. You need to start with the foundation and then work your way up.

This book covers everything from identifying your target audience to understanding the difference between an LLC and an S-Corporation, providing you with a solid foundation.

Chapter 1

Yes, There is Homework

Entrepreneurship isn't for everyone. Turning wonderful ideas into reality requires resilience and strong will. If you think being an entrepreneur means an easy and comfortable lifestyle, think again. The reality is full of struggles, hard work, and challenges.

Ask any successful entrepreneur; their journey is filled with moments of crippling self-doubt and one failed step after the other. It took them a while to even understand how business processes work and what they needed to do differently to gain an edge over their competitors.

To stand a chance in the highly competitive market, you need to be courageous and willing to learn every step of the way. Before you can dream about your life as an entrepreneur, you should ask yourself one basic question to make sure you're starting off on the right foot.

Why do you want to become an entrepreneur?

Is it because you hated your old job and realized you can't work for anyone? Or do you have a skill that needs to see the light of day? Or is it purely because starting a small business has recently become a trend that everyone seems to be partaking in?

These reasons alone won't suffice, and relying on them may jeopardize the longevity of your venture. If your decision to become an entrepreneur stems from frustration with a previous job, a desire for independence without a clear vision, or simply following a trend, your business may struggle to withstand the challenges ahead. Building a business requires a strong foundation grounded in purpose and principles.

When your business is built on strong principles, you can market it with conviction and strike a chord with your target audience. Your unwavering belief in your business idea and your business values will keep the wind in your sails. If you embark on the entrepreneurial journey for the wrong reasons, it becomes challenging to convince others to take you seriously.

However, if your motivation is to change the world with your innovative idea and you are committed to taking all the necessary steps, then you're on the right track. While the journey to success may be long and demanding, it becomes extremely fulfilling when you remain focused on your genuine business goals.

The Need for Market Research

When you're in the ideation phase, everything seems like a dream. You're open to a world of possibilities. You think that with the right resources and funds, your business idea will take off, and everything will go according to plan. But unfortunately, reality paints a different picture. It's important to be passionate about your business idea, but you can get sidetracked if you don't pay attention to the market.

You may think you have a million-dollar idea, but your target market may disagree. Some startups fail not because they did anything wrong, but because they picked the wrong time to launch their business. You need to be mindful of these little things that can keep your business from reaching its truest potential.

Before you can even begin conceptualizing your product or service or outlining your business plan, and devising marketing strategies, you need to do your homework. Dive into the market and collect as much information as possible about existing business practices to make informed decisions about your venture.

You might question the necessity of extensive market research. After all, it can be time-consuming and may seem like a hurdle delaying the realization of your business idea. While it's true that valuable insights often stem from personal failures, the truth is, you don't have to endure repeated setbacks to find success. Instead, you can leverage the experiences of failed businesses to learn and avoid common pitfalls. Market research holds significant importance for various reasons, and in the following sections, we'll explore the ways it can provide crucial lessons, allowing you to glean insights from the mistakes of others in the business world.

Finding Your Audience

Your idea is worth nothing if it isn't catering to an audience. There should be a market demand for your services, or there's no point in going forward. Even if you have a disruptive innovation, it's important for you to put out some feelers and see how people respond to it.

Dig deeper and figure out what problem you're trying to address in the market or if there is a market niche for your big idea. Testing the waters before taking the plunge is necessary because the losses end up being far greater than you've ever imagined.

Once you've identified your audience, you need to understand their preferences, needs, and habits to make sure you can sell your product or service to them effectively. Your business will only succeed if you do everything you can to please your target market.

Understanding Your Competitors

When several companies are doing what *you* plan to do, it's imperative that you study *their* business processes to devise a strategy that makes you stand out. Learn how their marketing plan can endanger yours and make sure you're able to withstand any external pressure by finding new ways to promote your product and gaining the upper hand.

When you're new in the game, you have an advantage. You can incorporate unique features into your product that will set you apart and take a different route with branding to earn a spot in the limelight.

Take Netflix, for example. The business's success can be attributed largely to first-mover advantage, as well as to careful competition analysis.

By closely studying the competition, such as Redbox and traditional cable TV providers, Netflix recognized the emerging trend of digital content consumption. They shifted their focus to streaming and invested in original content, giving them a significant competitive advantage.

Market research will allow you to set competitive prices for your products and cash in on your competitors' weaknesses by improving your own performance.

Managing Risks

Investing in a business is risky because you never know when things can go wrong. To manage risks involved with executing business decisions, you need to carry out detailed research and measure your chances of long-term survival. Your market research will help you make informed decisions and avoid risks when there isn't enough data to show evidence of success.

When you start a business equipped with the right knowledge and have an insight into how the market works, you'll be able to take calculated risks and minimize your losses.

Before diving headfirst into research, there are several things you need to consider ensuring you're not wasting your time looking at data that has no relevance to your business. Market research is necessary before you can formulate your business plan, but even before collecting the information, you need to figure out what you need to research and how. This can vary from business to business as what works for one might not work for the other.

Primary Objective

When you have a well-defined research objective, it'll be easier for you to find all the relevant information for your business. Don't set too many goals and keep them specific to the problem you're trying to solve and the market segment you're catering to. Your goals should be reasonable and realistic because sometimes, carrying out primary research isn't as simple as it seems. It can be expensive and difficult to obtain.

The purpose of an objective is to make sure your research produces conclusive results that you can use to come up with effective strategies and tackle the issues you wish to address with your business idea. Your research findings should help you get an in-depth understanding of how your business will unfold in the real world and the practical steps you need to take to ensure that it's profitable and sustainable in the long term.

Signs of a great objective are that it will make it clear to you whether you need to look at existing data or you need to collect the information by conducting surveys or interviews. It will also let you know if you need to study statistics and hard facts or if you need to focus on your potential consumers' emotions and feelings regarding the subject. The nature of your research ultimately depends on what you set out to achieve.

Defining research objectives is necessary for the early stages of starting a business because you can refer to them during the research process and make sure you're meeting your goals and not getting distracted by unnecessary information.

To ensure that your research is specific to your audience, you must select a large sample size for your surveys and questionnaires. The larger the data, the less room there is for errors. The data you collect should represent your target audience realistically.

Use stratified random sampling to make sure you're considering the needs and behavioral patterns of all kinds of people that will be interested in your product. In this method of sampling, you must divide the population into groups based on their shared interests, income, or their ethnicity, just to name a few. And then, you must select random people from each group to make sure your data includes a diverse group of people.

Stratified Random Sampling
https://www.simplypsychology.org/stratified-random-sampling.html]

Quantitative Data

Quantitative data is a numeric form of data that can be obtained from experiments, surveys, tests, market reports, and metrics. It's a lot easier to analyze because it's mostly structured and defined. It is mostly collected for explanatory research that seeks to give reasons for some of your business practices or product features. For e.g., the responses to a question like 'how much would you be willing to pay for this product' would allow you to price your product keeping your consumer's spending ability in mind.

Qualitative Data

Qualitative data, on the other hand, is more suited for exploratory research where you need to either discover trends or understand the reasons behind your consumer's buying habits and preferences. This type of data is typically used to explain quantitative data, to provide answers to a number of specific questions, or to decide the right questions to include in a survey, questionnaire, or focus group.

A question like 'what would you like to see as an added feature in this product' would let you explore all the different ways you can improve upon your product taking your consumer's preferences into consideration.

*[**Insert image 3 here Caption** Qualitative Data vs. Quantitative Data https://alicozzolinosmith.medium.com/quantitative-vs-qualitative-why-should-you-care-about-research-methods-47a24b576dc1]*

Methods of Research

After you've successfully defined your research goals and figured out if your business requires qualitative or quantitative data or a combination of both, you need to select the methods of research. But before we can explore each one of them, we must understand the two basic types of research these methods fall under.

1. Primary Research
2. Secondary Research

Primary Research

The purpose of conducting primary research is to find first-hand information that you cannot obtain from other existing resources. It's a costly measure as it involves figuring out what you need to learn, what method of research you'll have to employ, and what kind of questions you have to ask that'll yield the best results.

Even though it can be time-consuming or expensive, it is always specific to your research objectives. You won't have to examine useless information to learn something of substance for your business because it will already be tailored to your business needs.

Methods of primary research are as follows:

Interviews

You can conduct interviews to get expert advice and obtain qualitative data. These one-on-one meetings will allow you to gain a detailed insight into the lives of your target audience and truly understand their buyer's journey.

Questionnaires

Questionnaires consist of a set of questions that are used to obtain information that can be about certain consumer habits or product features. These are used just for the purpose of extracting data, not to draw a conclusion. Try to keep the questions to a minimum of 10 to make sure the response rate is high and people are able to answer all the questions honestly.

Surveys

Surveys are great for statistical analyses. They can be conducted to understand your brand awareness, how you can satisfy customers and earn their loyalty, and what kind of people are truly interested in buying your product.

They are one of the most used research methods because they allow you to understand your audience in the easiest way possible. Make sure your sample size is large and diverse enough to represent the majority of your target market.

User Groups

User groups are specific to businesses that offer an app or website as a service. To understand if the application is user-friendly, user groups are asked to give their feedback on its performance. Their recorded comments are largely responsible for influencing any design or functionality changes in the app or website to enhance the user experience.

Focus Groups

Focus groups are comprised of carefully selected individuals that are placed in a collaborative environment where they can bounce ideas off each other. It's important to gather people of different backgrounds and interests that are representative of different segments of your market to obtain a range of opinions and ideas.

Focus groups are a great resource to explore different advertising strategies or product features that would attract a larger number of consumers.

Secondary Research

Secondary research is a cost-effective method as it doesn't require you to conduct the research yourself. It relies on data obtained from previous studies, existing surveys, or questionnaires. To reach any conclusion, you must analyze the data according to your research goals and make sure the sample that was studied is relevant to your business as well.

Essentially, secondary research involves utilizing primary research conducted by other researchers. However, it is essential to invest time in finding material that aligns perfectly with your business goals. While secondary research can save costs, it comes with a critical caveat – ensure your sources are no older than 3 to 4 years.

Using outdated data poses a significant risk, as audience preferences, trends, and market dynamics evolve over time. The relevance and accuracy of your research heavily depend on the timeliness of the data. Emphasizing the importance of using up-to-date information is necessary to ensure that your business decisions are grounded in current market realities, thereby enabling you to stay ahead of the competition. Some methods of secondary research are:

Sales Data

By looking at competitive sales data, you can measure your business' success and see if you're reaching the targets that you had set for yourself(Blog.Hubspot, 2020). It is a great way to understand the market, your audience and learn where to direct your marketing strategies.

Competitor Benchmarks

Competitor benchmarks can be used to understand what your revenue and profit margin should be and if you need to increase your sales. They allow you to measure the growth metrics of your business as compared to your competitors.

Commercial Data

Commercial data is one form of secondary research that can be purchased to gain in-depth knowledge about industry trends.

Bottom Line

No matter what method you choose to go with for your business, you need to ask the right questions. Your market research should seek to answer the following questions honestly:

1. Who is your audience?
2. Which products do they purchase?
3. Why do they purchase those products?
4. How can you make them purchase your product?

When you've got a substantial number of responses, you can build your product and create your business plan accordingly. After you've done that successfully, there's nothing standing in the way of launching your product.

Even though research is a crucial part of starting a business, you need to narrow it down, or you'll end up wasting so much of your time studying and analyzing data that doesn't even directly relate to your business.

You can always hire a researcher, but with the internet at your disposal, you may not need to. Prioritize what's more valuable for your business so you can carry out a more focused market research and get straight down to business.

Chapter 2

Define the Target

There's no such thing as giving too much importance to your customers. You could have the most qualified workforce, the best products and services in the market, and the most generous investors, but if you miss crucial details about your customers, then all your marketing efforts will go down the drain. When you know your customers down to a T, you'll be able to formulate the most effective marketing strategies. Every step you take to serve your customers will work out in your favor in the long run.

Your customers and clients can be anyone from other businesses (B2B) to consumers (B2C) or both (B2B and B2C). If you don't put yourself in your customers' shoes and understand what their needs and preferences are, then how can you be sure that you're providing them the most amazing customer experience?

When you know your customers' demographics, characteristics, and behaviors, you can create targeted ad campaigns that will attract them to your products/services right away. You'll also be able to maintain strong customer relationships with them and possibly convert them into loyal customers. You must also identify their buying habits so that you can anticipate what they need before they learn about it themselves.

If you know anything about people, then you know they love to talk. Your consumers can spread the word about you if they feel valued and cared for when they approach you. The only way you can give them the kind of treatment they're looking for is by doing your research about them and making sure that you've gone over all the market segments.

You need to be careful when you're dealing with customers because they're not all the same. They have different goals, problems, and lifestyles. A marketing campaign that works for some may not work for others.

Like most things, it's better to document everything you know about your customers so that you know what to consider when you're reinventing your marketing strategies or altering something about your brand.

Buyer Persona

A buyer persona is a fictional representation of your prospective customers. It's prepared after intense market research and by looking at actual data of your current customers. To have a clearly defined target customer, you need to prepare the most elaborate buyer persona. One great thing about it is that it humanizes the customer on the other end and makes you realize the need to develop truly engaging content to retain all your customers.

This document has all the information you could need—demographic information, hobbies, family size, and history. It's a way to learn all about your audience, what motivates them, and the challenges they face every day. When you know your customers so well, you'll be able to create marketing messages that speak to their souls and get them interested in your brand right away.

You need to include the following items about your potential buyers in your buyer persona:

- Location
- Age
- Gender
- Education
- Hobbies
- Job title
- Income bracket
- Relationship status
- Goals
- Challenges
- Beliefs
- Needs
- Social circle
- Behavior

To create buyer personas, you need to first learn everything you can about your customers through online research, surveys, and interviews. After you've gathered all that information, you have to segment them based on their shared interests, beliefs, needs, etc.

Let's consider an example for a fictional company, "Healthy Bites," which specializes in organic snacks and wellness products.

Buyer Persona – Sarah Health-Conscious:

Demographics:

- Age: 32
- Location: Urban area
- Gender: Female
- Education: College graduate

Lifestyle and Interests:

- Hobbies: Yoga, hiking, cooking
- Family Size: Married with one child
- Job Title: Marketing Manager
- Income Bracket: Middle to upper-middle class

Personal Goals:

- Maintain a healthy lifestyle
- Provide nutritious snacks for her family

Challenges:

- Limited time for extensive meal preparation
- Balancing work and family commitments

Beliefs:

- Values organic and sustainable products
- Prioritizes wellness and mindful living

Needs:

- Convenient and healthy snack options
- Reliable information on product ingredients and sourcing

Social Circle:

- Engages with online wellness communities
- Follows health and nutrition influencers on social media

Behavior:

- Shops online for organic and eco-friendly products
- Seeks product reviews and recommendations

Internal Sources of Research

Contact Databases

Look through your contact databases to obtain a wealth of information about your customers. You can also discover trends about how your customers learn about you and consume your products and services.

Feedback from Sales and Customer Service Teams

Ask your sales team for their feedback on the type of customers they interact with the most and see if any generalizations can be formed. Your customer service team also knows a great deal about your buyer's needs and preferences so you need to collect as much data from them as you can to create the most realistic buyer personas.

Site Analytics

If you own an online business, then you should use site analytics tools to assess whatever you can about the behavior of your customers (Rai, 2019). Site analytics is basically the process of analyzing the behavior of visitors to your website. You can use this to learn all the steps your customers took before they chose to buy your product/service and get their demographic data as well, such as their age, location, or device they're using.

Customer Surveys

The reason why so many companies have incomplete buyer personas is that their surveys are capturing wrong information and that's worse than having no information. Customers fill them out half-heartedly and aren't completely honest with their answers because these surveys are usually prepared haphazardly and don't ask the right questions.

Surveys are supposed to help you understand who your customers are, what they need, and what kind of problems they face every day. They should allow you to pick your customer's brains so that you can base your personas on real people and not just ideas of them. A good survey needs to have some open-ended questions as well because they'll provide additional insight into who your customers are and what they value.

The first thing you need to do before preparing a survey is to ask yourself what you wish to achieve as a result of this. When you have a clear goal in mind, you'll be able to tailor the questions accordingly.

The order of questions is equally as important as what's being asked. If you ask complicated questions right off the bat, then it won't take long for your customers to lose all their interest. Begin by asking warm-up questions with multiple-choice or rate-scale answers that are less time-consuming.

After getting the easier questions out of the way, you can segue into more challenging questions that seek to find the information you couldn't have obtained through secondary research. End the survey with easier demographic questions or leave space for additional comments to bring it full circle.

A good practice is to be upfront and state how long the survey will take on the very first page. The last thing you want to do is waste your customer's precious time. Also, be transparent about what you wish to do with the findings, so they feel like they've contributed to something useful.

If you need to get deeper insights to build a better buyer persona then make sure your survey answers the following questions about your consumers:

- What drives their behavior?
- What are their expectations?
- What are the obstacles they face while purchasing a product?

After you've received more than enough responses, you can start segmenting them. We'll go into more detail about that later in this chapter.

Interviews

Interviews are a great way to get to the bottom of what drives your target audience so you can develop the perfect buyer personas. There are different types of people you need to interview to get the most accurate findings of your customer base.

The number of people you need to interview depends on your market segment, but it's advisable to interview at least three people for each buyer persona that you're creating. Try to select them from a diverse group of people to make sure you're not missing anything crucial about your audience.

You'll know when to stop interviewing people when you start predicting how the interviewees are going to respond to your answers. When these patterns start becoming apparent and you know what to expect, then you can move on to the next phase.

Existing Customers

The best people to interview are your existing customers. They're familiar with your company and they're the closest and most realistic representations of your target customers. Make sure you have a mix of both satisfied and unsatisfied customers so that you can get a clearer understanding of your personas.

Only interviewing people who love your product is not going to help you identify what's wrong with your products and how you can do better. Customers who aren't impressed with your products or services will let you know what you need to do to engage them and what seems to be lacking. You'll also learn about their challenges and figure out ways your business can help them.

Most customers want to be listened to and conducting interviews with them will make them feel involved in your business. As a result, they may become loyal to your business and spread the word about you. So not only will you be gaining useful information, but you could also be making customers for life.

Prospective Customers

You also need to interview people who aren't familiar with your brand at all and haven't bought any of your products or services. Their input will help you understand your prospective customers more in-depth and you'll realize what you need to do or do differently to attract more customers. A fresh perspective is useful because it allows you to see your products and services in a new light and spot the flaws that you couldn't see before. It also lets you form a better and more inclusive judgment of your potential clientele.

Recruiting Interviewees

To get a better response rate for your interviews, you need to offer your interviewees an incentive to get them interested. Something as simple as an Amazon gift card could work depending on your customer's buying habits.

When you're dealing with non-customers, then you need to be especially honest about what you wish to achieve from your session with them and let them know that it's nothing like a sales call. No one likes being forced into buying something and chances are your interviewees won't turn up if they don't know what they've been called in for right from the get-go. Tell them that you only wish to learn from them so that you can understand your audience better and improve the quality of your products and services.

Try to work around their schedule if it's not too much trouble. Ask them to pick the time they're most comfortable with. When you're accommodating and understanding, it'll be a lot easier for them to say yes to you after you've approached them. They'll come in with an open mind and will be more forthcoming with their responses and feedback.

What You Need to Ask

The interview should involve a good mix of questions if you wish to create complete persona profiles that accurately depict all your customer segments.

Personal Background

Ask them about their age, relationship status, education, the schools they attended, and how they ended up where they are today.

Company

Include a handful of questions about the company they work for and the industry they're a part of if they're employed.

Role

Ask about their role in the company, who they report to, who reports to them, and any skills they need to have to do their job, etc.

Goals

It's also important to learn about their goals and what success means to them.

Challenges

Ask them about their biggest challenges in both their personal and professional life. Their answers will allow you to see how your business can be of help to them.

Shopping Preferences

Ask them what they prefer in their shopping experience, how they'd like to interact with vendors (e.g. phone, email, or in-person), what they look for in terms of quality when they're buying a product, etc.

Instead of just getting the questions out of the way, it's important to dig deeper and ask them why they feel the way that they do. Interviews are conducted to learn about things that can't be measured or obtained with a simple survey or site analytics tools. They help you put faces to the names and numbers you're used to seeing, allowing you to get more creative and thoughtful when you're coming up with newer marketing strategies for your business.

It's not just about gaining customers or getting a lot of visitors to your website. It's about retaining them too. You'll have greater chances of making your customers loyal to your brand if you prepare your products and deliver your services keeping their challenges and goals in mind and making sure your business is doing its part in making their lives easier.

Using Your Research to Create Buyer Personas

After you've done all your research and gathered a substantial amount of information, it's time to use it to create your buyer personas. Since you have raw, unorganized data, you need to figure out a way to make it understandable for yourself first before you can organize it to find patterns and commonalities in all the responses.

You can have more than one persona if your target audience spans a diverse group of people with different interests, backgrounds, income brackets, and age groups. These personas can then be used to guide your marketing plans to catch the attention of a wider group of people.

While there isn't a strict limit to the number of buyer personas you can create, it's essential to strike a balance. The goal is to ensure that your marketing efforts remain focused and effective. Several factors determine the appropriate number of buyer personas:

1. **Audience Diversity:** If your target audience is highly diverse, with distinct segments that have significantly different needs and preferences, creating multiple personas can be beneficial. Each persona should represent a unique segment of your audience.
2. **Resource Constraints:** The number of personas you create should align with your resources, both in terms of time and budget. Developing and implementing targeted marketing strategies for each persona requires resources, so it's essential to be realistic about what your team can manage effectively.

3. **Marketing Goals:** Consider your marketing objectives. If your goal is to penetrate various market segments with tailored messages, having multiple personas may be appropriate. However, if your focus is on a specific niche, a more targeted approach with fewer personas might be sufficient.
4. **Data Availability:** The accuracy and effectiveness of your personas depend on the quality of the data you have. If you lack sufficient data to create distinct and well-defined personas, it might be better to focus on a smaller number until more data becomes available.

In general, start with a manageable number of personas that cover the most significant segments of your audience. As your business evolves and you gather more data, you can refine or expand your personas to better align with your growing understanding of your customers.

Once you've arranged your research in a way that makes sense to you and you're able to find characteristics that can be grouped together, it'll be very easy to create a buyer persona. For example, you notice that a sizable number of people, who filled out the survey or visited your website the most, are middle-aged women who also happen to be pet owners. This information can be taken and turned into a persona.

Here's how you can do that. Come up with a name for your buyer, a job title, an address, and other defining characteristics that would reflect your findings accurately. It should seem like the profile of a real person, but it shouldn't be too specific. It should have as much information as you can gather about a person from a short conversation on a plane. Don't forget to include the goals and pain points too as they will help you come up with strategies that will resonate with your audience on a deeper level.

You should include real-life quotes from your interviews as well to paint a clearer picture and even add a list of objections they might raise when you contact them. When you share this persona with the sales team, they'll be more equipped to address and respond to anything that comes up during their conversations with the clients.

A persona is more than just a group of characteristics. It represents a segment of your target customers and it won't necessarily match every single characteristic of your customers. But it's enough to give you an idea about the kind of people you'll be catering to and interacting with daily so you can be fully prepared to handle all kinds of queries and complaints.

Value Proposition

A value proposition is a statement that explains how your business adds value to the lives of your customers and ultimately convinces your potential customers to choose you over your competitors. A good value proposition helps your prospects identify what makes your business the best provider for a particular product or service.

An effective value proposition should be convincing enough to turn your potential customers into loyal customers. It's often the first thing your customers notice when they hear about your brand, so it needs to be clear, concise, and impactful.

The value proposition canvas is a tool you can use to make sure your value proposition is centered around the values of your customers.

It includes the following items:

- Customer segment
- Persona
- Jobs to Be Done
- Pains
- Gains
- Products and Services
- Pain Relievers
- Gain Creators
- Value Proposition

Customer Segment

Your customer segment is the audience you're targeting with your products and services. They can be industry-based, demographic, geographic, behavioral, etc.

Persona

Your buyer's persona, as we've established in this chapter, describes who your customer is. This includes their profession, background, demographics, characteristics, goals, and challenges.

Jobs to Be Done

Jobs to be done are basically the needs of your customers. What are the jobs that your customer is trying to do in their professional or personal life? These can be a combination of emotional, functional, and social.

Pains

Pains are the problems that your customers are facing and keeping them from getting their jobs done.

Gains

Gains are what make your customers happy. They're the outcomes that your customers are expecting, and they can be functional and/or financial.

Products and Services

This is the solution you've chosen to provide your customers to help them get their jobs done and add value to their lives.

Pain Relievers

Pain relievers are practical components of your business that solve the problems your customers are facing.

Gain Creators

Gain creators are everything your business does to help your customers achieve their gains and overcome the challenges they face in their day-to-day lives.

Value Proposition

Your value proposition refers to the strongest values you promise to deliver to your customers if they choose to buy your products/services. You can use your value proposition statement as a business or marketing statement to summarize how your company solves the problems of your customers.

Bottom Line

It's crucial for your business to have a deep understanding of your customers. This knowledge will enable you to reach out to your target audience effectively. To attract customers and retain them for a long time, it's necessary to understand what motivates them. By paying attention to their needs and challenges, you can provide them with the best solutions. Otherwise, they'll look for another company that can meet their requirements. The satisfaction of your customers is vital for the growth and success of your business. Even if you do everything else right, ignoring their desires can lead to failure.

Chapter 3

The Purpose of It All

The vision, mission, and cultural statements are crucial components of any business. They provide a concise description of your key activities, how you wish to add value to your customers' lives, where you're headed, and how you plan to reach your ultimate destination.

Before you can get started on conceptualizing your vision, mission, and cultural statements, you need to learn the difference between all three.

Vision Statement

Your vision statement is the driving force that motivates you to achieve your business goals. It defines your most important targets but doesn't include a practical plan to achieve those targets.

The vision statement encompasses everything from how you plan to help your customers and offer value to the world with your products and services to everything you hope to achieve as a business.

It can be anywhere from a few sentences to several paragraphs long and needs to be written in plain language that will resonate with you, your employees, and your customers. It should be aspirational, inspirational, and motivational.

Here is an example of a vision statement:

"At [Company Name], our vision is to become a global leader in sustainable technology solutions. We aspire to revolutionize the way people live and work by providing innovative, eco-friendly products and services that enhance the quality of life. Through our commitment to environmental stewardship and cutting-edge technology, we envision a world where sustainability and progress coexist harmoniously, leaving a lasting positive impact on future generations."

Mission Statement

A mission statement, on the other hand, is a lot more practical. It describes the course of action your business needs to take every day to turn your vision statement into a reality.

Your mission statement will serve as guidance when you're formulating new strategies for your business. You need to make sure your mission statement has a practical focus, is based in the present, and explains exactly why your business exists to members of your organization and anyone else who's interested in your business. Since it's based on a practical plan, it's a lot easier to write than a vision statement.

Your mission statement should be written in such a way that it uplifts and inspires you when you're feeling lost and searching for ways to get your business back on track. It should be short, clear, and impactful.

Here is an example of a mission statement:

"Our mission at [Company Name] is to empower individuals and businesses through accessible and efficient financial solutions. We strive to deliver unparalleled financial services that cater to the unique needs of our clients. By fostering a culture of innovation, transparency, and client-centricity, we aim to create lasting value and contribute to the financial well-being of our customers. Every day, we dedicate ourselves to providing actionable insights and personalized solutions, ensuring the financial success of those we serve."

Cultural Statement

Cultural statements are much like mission statements, except they're internal. They're written for your employees. They provide an insight into your company's principles, objectives, values, and how all members of the organization are expected to interact with one another.

Here is an example of a cultural statement:

> "At [Company Name], our culture is built on collaboration, continuous learning, and a shared passion for innovation. We believe in fostering an environment where every team member is empowered to contribute their unique skills and perspectives. Our commitment to open communication, respect, and inclusivity defines our workplace ethos. We embrace diversity as a strength and cultivate a culture that values teamwork, creativity, and individual growth. Together, we strive to create a workplace that not only achieves professional excellence but also nurtures a sense of belonging and fulfillment for all our employees."

These statements can vary by length and structure and should accurately depict an organization's way of life. Also, when you're writing all three statements, it's important for you to understand your company's unique selling proposition first. Make sure your business values are clear and precise, so you can look to them for inspiration and create statements that are concise yet engaging.

Bottom Line

The mission and vision statements of your business are crucial declarations that provide it with an identity and structure. These statements define the central purpose of your organization and create a sense of belonging in the employees. Together with your cultural statement, these statements give new employees a mission to look forward to. They create a unique sense of identity for your company and ensure that only individuals who abide by these statements end up working for your firm.

Chapter 4

Brand Matters

One of the most exciting things about starting a business has to do with naming it. Finding a name that fits your business perfectly and isn't a mouthful to pronounce is something most people already know. But sometimes, even if you've spent a lot of time and effort in coming up with your business name, your business can still get lost amongst the competitors simply because there was nothing memorable about it.

Naming your business is one of the first steps you take when you're about to launch your business because you need to make sure it's available as a domain name. But you should never do it in a rush. Get other people's opinions too if you can, because their fresh perspective can help you discard names that may hold meaning to you but won't necessarily make sense to the rest of the world.

Choosing a great name may seem like pure luck because you never know what name resonates with your audience. Google, for example, isn't just some random word they picked out of nowhere. It's a playful twist on the word 'googol', which is a number with a 1 followed by a 100 zeros.

It clearly represents what the brand does i.e. organize the vast amount of information available on the internet, and is a simple and memorable name. So much so, in fact, that it has stopped being *just* a brand, and is also used as a verb, meaning to make an online search.

But this approach may not work for everyone. A simple name that's already a part of your vernacular can do wonders for your business too. Sometimes it can take seconds for you to come up with a catchy name, and other times, it can take months, and you still won't come across a name that sounds perfect to your ears.

Why does it matter?

But what's in a name? How can a combination of letters dictate your company's future?

It's a Gateway to Your Company

In a way, your company name is the gateway to your company. It's the first thing people see or hear. If it doesn't stick, then you might as well rename your business, and that's a completely different process on its own. To make a good first impression, you need to come up with the perfect name for your business that stands out but isn't completely unheard of.

It Represents What Your Company Stands For

Another reason why it matters is that it represents all that a company stands for. When people hear a name, and it seems like it wasn't given much thought, then they're likely to assume that the business owner isn't too concerned about their business.

Your name should truly sum up everything your company is about, and it should also be appropriate for your industry. For example, Cami Cakes is a great name for a bakery but not for a lawyer's office. Be mindful of the industry you're targeting during your brainstorming.

It Increases Your Chances of Gaining Traction

If your business name is so interesting that it grabs people's attention right away, then chances are that they're already interested in you, and this will work well for you if your product lives up to their expectations as well.

Finding the Perfect Brand Name

Select the Type

Before you can begin the process of naming your brand, it is crucial to define the type of name that will best align with your business identity and goals. Each type of brand name carries distinct characteristics, influencing how your audience perceives your business.

Below, we'll explore various types of brand names – such as descriptive, acronymic, associative, suggestive, eponymous, invented, or non-English – each with its unique advantages and considerations. By understanding these types, you can make an informed decision that not only reflects your brand essence but also positions you strategically in the market.

Descriptive

Descriptive brand names convey exactly what the company is all about. The great thing about a name like this is that your target audience won't have to dig around to find out about the kind of services you offer. It will be apparent right from the start. Home Depot is the perfect example of this as the name makes it obvious what you can find at the store.

But the downside of having such a name is that if you wish to diversify your brand down the line, the name will no longer fit perfectly.

Acronymic

Sometimes the acronym of a name can sound great as a company name. So, if you've thought of a name that seems like the right fit for your business but is a mouthful to pronounce, try playing with just the initials to see if it sounds any better. Some renowned brand names of this type are NASA, IBM, IKEA, etc.

But some acronyms can be hard to remember if you have to pronounce each letter separately. It has worked for IBM because they have been around for so long, but it may not work for you if you're just starting out.

Associative

If you wish to add meaning to your business name, then you should pick an associative name for your business and create relevance with something that's known for its unique properties or traits. Amazon, the name of the world's largest ecommerce website, is a great associative name because the world's largest river is also called the Amazon.

Name your company after something that matches up with your business objectives as well. The last thing you want to do is make people wonder why you chose a name that doesn't showcase what your business is actually about in the least bit.

Suggestive

Suggestive names are different from descriptive names in that they simply allude to the features of the products and services that are being offered. They're less direct, which makes them an ideal choice for you if you wish to change up your brand in the future.

One great example of a suggestive name is UBER. The word means 'an outstanding example', so it goes well for a company with big goals. Facebook, a combination of two words, is also another example of this.

Eponymous

Many businesses are named after their founders like Disney, Carl Zeiss, Tom Ford, and Chanel. The upside to naming your brand after yourself is that they are less likely to be taken by someone else. They are safe and can be easily trademarked.

But if your name isn't the easiest to pronounce, then you must consider another type of business name.

Invented

If you've tried your hardest to find an existing word that would fit your business and failed, then just make one up. Make sure the name you've coined is distinctive enough to catch attention and is easy to say. You can assign a meaning to these names yourself, and it won't be a problem at all to trademark them.

You can take inspiration from Greek Mythology or even Latin roots and come up with a fancy name of your own. Some popular examples of invented brand names are Verizon and Xerox.

Non-English

You don't have to pick a name that has a basis in the English language. If you're allowed to make up a name, then you can definitely derive your brand name from non-English languages. You may be surprised to know that Samsung is actually a Korean word meaning 'three stars'.

The most important and popularly used types of brand names have been mentioned above, but there are a few others like geographical or historical that can also be considered if they'd work well for your business.

After selecting the type of name, you can start brainstorming ideas for your business name. There are a couple of ways to go about this. It's better to have a plan than to randomly decide a name and go with it. You have to make sure the name stands out and that you won't change your mind about it. Your team should also unanimously agree on the name to avoid any conflicts later on.

Make a List

Before you can think of names, start by listing down all the attributes you want your brand to be associated with. Write down any adjectives that you can think of that would best describe the experience you're going to deliver and how you'd want people to feel about your business. Think of your customers and try to figure out what kind of business values they'll be looking for.

After you're done putting all of these words on paper, come up with the names that reflect these words in the best way. It's not possible to find a name that would represent all of the words you've penned down. With every name you come up with, check off the items on that list that inspired it.

Prioritize the items that are most important for your business and see if the names convey most of them perfectly.

Make Sure There's a Connection

It's not just about finding a name that sounds right. You've got to make sure it will resonate with your audience too. If your business allows for it, then you can build an emotional connection with your customers. Think of names that will induce an emotional response in people.

But if your business deals with something purely functional, then you need to find attention-grabbing names that will clearly convey how you're solving a problem for the consumers.

If there's a story or concept behind your business, that can be a great way to form a long-lasting relationship with your customers.

Narrow Them Down

After you've come up with as many names representing your brand, you need to figure out a way to narrow it down.

Go through the list and discard the names that seem too long or too confusing for the general audience. Names that are too short may not accurately deliver the values your business is built upon so you may have to get rid of them too.

Once you've narrowed them down to a handful of names, you can ask your team and decide which one is the most accurate fit for your business.

Put Out Feelers

After you've agreed upon a name, test it out on your friends, family, acquaintances, or investors to see how they respond to it. One way to get the most genuine reactions out of them is to not tell them what it is. Casually bring the name up in a conversation and observe their expressions. If you're met with interested and curious looks, then the name might work for you. But if they respond with incredulous or confused expressions, then chances are the name isn't good enough, and you'll have to go back to the drawing board.

After you've found a name that you love the most out of all the options, check if it isn't already taken before you start putting out feelers about it. If you find out that it's not available to use after everybody around you has expressed genuine excitement for it, then it might kill your hopes, and you may feel like there's no other name that you'd like better.

You need to be patient during the brainstorming process because finding the perfect name is really important for your business, and it can take time. Don't settle for a name because you may grow to hate it, and it's not a good sign for your business if you can't even say the name with confidence.

Now that we've gone over all the do's, let's discuss some of the don'ts of naming your business.

Don'ts of Naming Your Business

The name of your business is the first steppingstone. If something doesn't match up, it will put your business at major risk in the years to come because getting people to remember your brand name is the first step you need to take before you can think about converting them into potential customers.

There are many mistakes to avoid while coming up with names for your business. Some of them are listed below.

Don't Get Everyone Involved

Now it's true that two minds are better than one, but when you involve so many people with different tastes and preferences, it can get especially difficult to reach an agreement. When you're trying to please everyone and paying attention to what everyone has to say, whether they're your family members or friends, then you can lose sight of your own objectives and get distracted easily.

It's important to only select a handful of people who you trust and are personally involved in your business instead of letting every random person influence your decision. When so many people are allowed a say in the naming process, you may end up with a name that's very bland and safe.

But you shouldn't play it safe. You need to make a bold statement with your brand name, even if you have to upset a few people who don't agree with your choice. If you don't want to alienate people, it's advised to keep only a few people on your team who will offer sensible advice to you if you get too carried away.

Don't Use Boring Words

Do you know what never works as a brand name? Something that people won't even register as a brand name. It may work if you're the only company in your city or country that offers a service, but when you have competition, you need to make every effort to stand out and get people interested.

But what counts as a boring name?

A boring name states the obvious. It's like calling your bakery 'baked goods'. With so many amazing name ideas around the world, settling with a boring name won't serve your business well.

Take all the time you need to come up with an interesting, eye-catching name, or you'll be forgotten by your target audience very soon. All your branding and marketing efforts won't save your company because the very thing that's supposed to stick out about your business doesn't evoke any feeling.

Don't Make It Too Vague

You may not know that the name you've picked out for your business is too obscure until you find people struggling to pronounce it or looking up the meaning of the word. It may be very close to your heart and represent something special, but if other people can't see that just by hearing the word, you need to think of another one.

It's good to have a story behind the name, but it should be understandable to the general public. Try not to name your company as a Spanish or French phrase that's hard to pronounce. It may have a beautiful meaning, but it'll lose its relevance if people can't even say it right.

For some businesses, working with a name that's a little obscure can work. Hulu, for example, is the name of an online video streaming website. It's a Mandarin word with two meanings: interactive recording and gourd, but it doesn't sound unnatural because there are only a few popular streaming services, so the founders did what they had to do to draw attention. But when you're one of the thousands in the market, you need to be careful with strange names.

Don't Change the Spelling

Sometimes, after you finalize a name, a simple Google search reveals that the name is already trademarked. In these desperate times, try not to change the spelling of your company name just to keep it. It will end up looking more like the name of a prescription drug than anything else.

Using a 'K' instead of 'Q' or 'F' instead of 'PH' not only makes your company look tacky, but it can become harder to discover online. If a customer heard about your company through a friend and typed the name into Google to learn more about it, it's highly unlikely that they will purposefully try to misspell it.

It's better to invent a name than to misspell it. Misspelling the name worked out well for Google, but that's because they were the only one in the game offering that level of service. The only way you can market your company with a misspelled name is if you have a large marketing budget and pull out all the stops in your branding efforts.

Building Your Brand

When you own a small business, you don't think of it as a brand. That's because people usually associate the word 'brand' with large companies that have enormous marketing budgets and national or even global recognition. It becomes especially difficult to think about your business in those terms when you look at established giants like Nike, Amazon, and Starbucks.

But to put it simply, a brand is an idea or image that comes to your mind when you think about a specific company or its products/services. It's more than just about the physical features; it's also about the emotions you develop towards the company and its products.

Branding is important for all kinds of businesses because it adds value to a company's image, and it gives the employees a sense of direction. With the right brand concept, you'll be able to make and retain new customers for your business easily.

Then there's marketing. While branding establishes the 'why' of the business, marketing defines the 'how'. It's all about making active efforts to promote your brand and reaching your target audience. Marketing seeks to gain leads and sales for your business and branding builds your company's reputation and strengthens customer loyalty. The two may seem like different concepts but they're interrelated.

With great branding, your conversions will also significantly improve. It will also add meaning to your marketing strategies which is better for your business in the long run because you'll be making a difference in people's lives independent of purchase.

Now that we know that branding is more than just the colors and the logo of your company, we can start thinking about how you can create a distinctive identity for your business and trigger an emotional response in your consumers.

To build a strong brand, you need to work on the face, personality and values promoted by your business. You need to cover every area, from your company's social media profile to the packaging of your products and the delivery of your services.

A good brand reflects the people behind the business, what they believe in and how they wish to be perceived by people. You'll know you're going in the right direction if your brand delivers the message behind your business clearly, if it makes you look credible, and encourages your audience to take the next step, i.e. buy your product/service.

Define Your Brand

The first thing you need to do is define clearly what your brand is all about. When you establish your brand values in the beginning, you'll be able to come up with marketing strategies that effectively communicate them to your audience.

You can do this by simply noting down everything that's close to your heart and reflects what your company stands for (your mission and vision). If you care about the environment, then you can take the necessary steps like using recyclable equipment and carrying out tree plantation drives to let the world know that the choices you make align with your values and reaffirm your credibility as a business.

Defining your brand can be overwhelming because everything else that follows will rely heavily on what you've established here. To make sure you're on the right track, answer the following questions.

- What's your brand mission?
- What do you offer the world?
- What do you want people to think of your business?
- What are the qualities that you wish people associate with your business?

It's necessary for you to do your research before finalizing everything. Understand your audience by analyzing your buyer personas and figure out ways to attract customers. Learn about their values, needs, and challenges, and then create your brand mission.

Understanding Color Theory, Meaning &Psychology

You need to understand the basic principles of color theory to get the colors right for your company.

The 12-step color wheel that was developed by Isaac Newton will help you choose the perfect colors for your company. Colors affect the way we feel about certain things which is why they're used quite strategically in design and advertising to influence our feelings about products.

For example, the blue color is known to have calming effects on your mind. A meditation app can make use of this color to attract its target audience. Some colors are also known to increase your metabolism and raise your blood pressure.

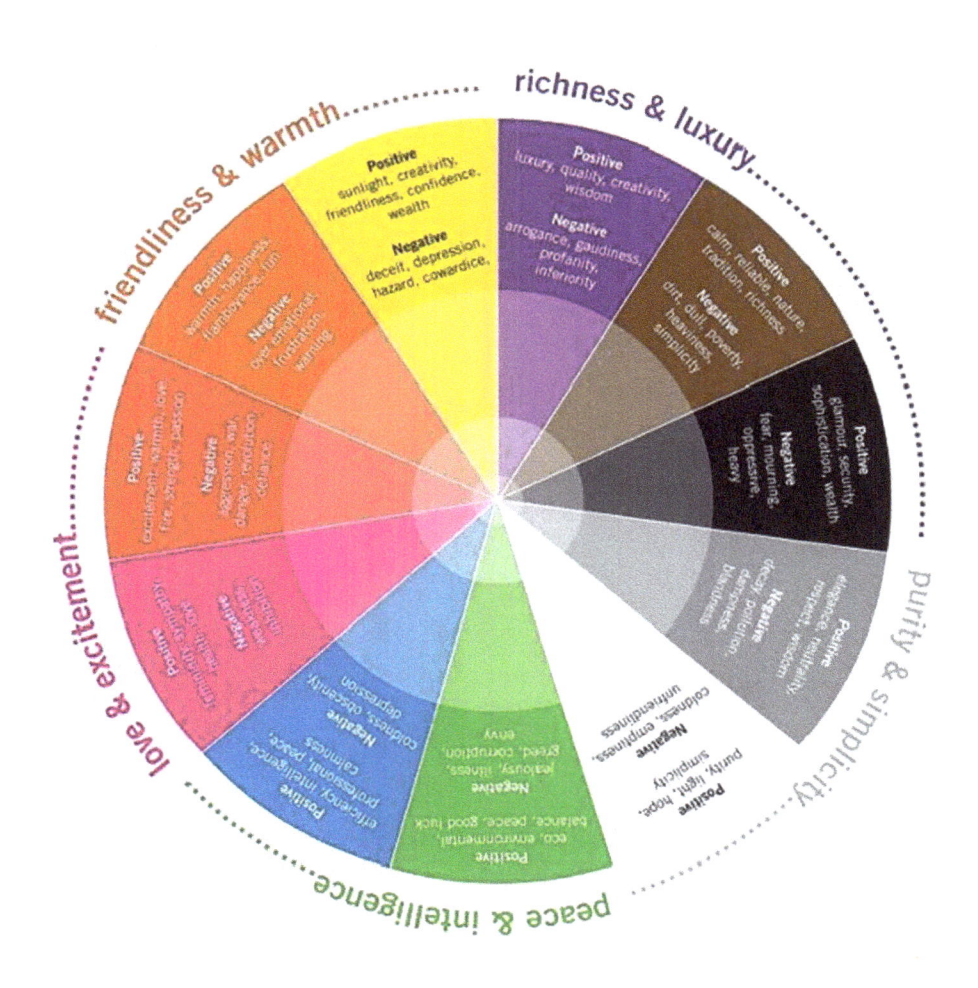

Let's take a look at a few colors and what they represent:

Red: Energy, ambition, passion, determination, anger, and sexual passion
Orange: Optimism and social communication
Yellow: Cheerfulness and optimism
Green: Balance, growth, and self-reliance
Blue: Trust, peace, loyalty, and integrity
Indigo: Intuition, idealism, and structure
Purple: Imagination, creativity, and individualism
Turquoise: Communication and clarity of mind
Pink: Unconditional love and nurturing
Brown: Friendly, down-to-earth, security, and comfort
Gray: Compromise and intellect
Silver: Fluidity, emotion, sensitivity, and mystery
Gold: Success, triumph, luxury, prosperity, and achievement
White: Completeness, purity, and perfection
Black: Hidden, unknown, and secretive

Depending on the kind of effect you wish to have on your prospective customers, you can design your products, website, and application with the appropriate colors to elicit the desired response from your audience.

The color wheel allows you to choose a combination of colors that go together perfectly and help with readability as well. Complementary colors are placed directly across each other on the wheel. If there isn't enough contrast between two colors that have been used with each other, then it can create visual vibrations, causing discomfort to your eyes.

If you're unsure if you have the right contrast, then you need to squint and look at the colors again. If the colors start turning grey and blend in with each other, that means you need more contrast. You may have to adjust the color values to create better contrast.

Be Consistent

Once you've picked out the colors that most accurately reflect the essence of your company, you need to make sure you use them consistently with your business. Your audience should be able to recognize your brand before even reading your name because of the colors.

When you think about recognizable brands like Facebook and Coca-Cola, you don't even have to think twice to remember the colors they've used. That's the kind of effect you must seek to create. If you have a website, make sure the theme is consistent with your color scheme.

Your logo, banners, and background should also be designed using the main brand colors. You can deviate from the theme for marketing campaigns, one-off events, and your social media posts as well because too much consistency can make your social media presence look uninteresting.

Establish a Voice for Your Company

Your tone of voice is equally as important as everything else. It's how you communicate your message to the world and market your products and services. Depending on your industry, it can be professional, casual, or funny and it should strike a chord with your target audience.

As an owner of a business-to-business (B2B) firm, you'll need to keep your tone formal and make sure all your content follows that route. If you're a friendly pet store, then you can use a conversational tone of voice.

All your written content like your blogs, captions, tweets, should use your brand's voice as well. To help you content creators stay within the branding guidelines, prepare a document and share it with everyone.

Stay consistent across all your social media and marketing channels.

Increase Sales with Marketing Materials

Your business also needs to have printed materials prepared carefully to promote your products and services. These include newsletters, brochures, catalogs, letterheads, business cards, and many more. While you may possess artistic flair, it may be a better idea to hire professionals such as advertising agencies or a graphic designers to create these for you.

The expertise of an advertising agency or graphic designer brings a level of finesse to your marketing materials that goes beyond artistic ability. These professionals understand the nuances of effective communication and brand representation. By hiring them, you can ensure that your materials not only showcase your products and services but also resonate with your target audience in the cleanest and most professional manner possible.

One crucial advantage of professional assistance lies in sticking to fundamental design principles. Skilled designers understand the importance of layout, color schemes, typography, and overall visual hierarchy. Neglecting these principles can lead to a less-than-optimal presentation, potentially requiring costly reprints. By collaborating with experts, you mitigate the risk of design errors, saving both time and resources.

Moreover, hiring professionals allows you to avoid overloading your materials with unnecessary information. Skilled designers can strike the right balance between conveying essential details and maintaining readability. They can adeptly break up text with illustrations, photos, and charts, ensuring that your audience engages with the content seamlessly.

In essence, while your artistic instincts may be commendable, the advantages of professional expertise in marketing material design are significant. Investing in the services of an advertising agency or a skilled graphic designer not only elevates the visual appeal of your materials but also ensures a strategic and effective representation of your brand in the market.

Bottom Line

To achieve success in business, starting the right way is crucial. The first step towards building a strong brand image is to come up with a perfect name that truly represents your business. However, it is important to ensure that the name you choose is not already trademarked. Additionally, you must also check if the corresponding domain name is available so that you can set up your website and make it easy for your potential customers to find you online.

If you realize that your chosen name is not working out for your business in the initial months, it's alright to change it. It's important to keep experimenting and find a name that resonates with your target audience and is memorable.

So, it's time to unleash your creativity and brainstorm a name that truly reflects your business and leaves a lasting impression on your potential customers.

Chapter 5

The Legal Stuff

When you first start conceptualizing your business, you're focused on branding, marketing strategies, and product design. You don't pay much attention to how you will execute everything and all the paperwork that needs to be filed before establishing a business.

But when you're finally about to bring your ideas to life, reality hits you, and you realize there's so much to get right before you can even think about getting your first few customers. Choosing the right business structure and learning about all the taxes you'll have to pay as a small business can be overwhelming before you've even stepped foot into the entrepreneurial lifestyle.

You need to realize that you can't launch your business overnight. You'll have to consider all the legalities to plan out your finances accordingly. But the first thing on the roadmap to successfully launching your company is picking the right business structure because that'll impact your overall taxes and distribution of profits.

Establish a Legal Business Structure

Having a formal business structure is essential as it affects the monetary aspects of your business. Your choice of business structure can depend on what you're planning to get out of it. It can allow you to lower what you pay in taxes, separate your personal assets from your business, and be considered a legitimate business. It can also have a significant role to play in your fundraising plans.

But figuring out what type of business structure is ideal for your business is no easy task. Let's go into the most common entities in detail so you can understand what will work for your business. It's advised to consult an accountant or a lawyer who has dealt with businesses in the past. They'll guide you through this process and help you make an informed decision. Don't take your chances on this one because if it doesn't work out, it will cost you a lot of money down the line.

Corporation

For small businesses, forming a corporation might not be the smartest thing to do because they're very complex. If you have a very small team of employees or work with a partner, you should consider other business structures. It's ideal for larger companies with many employees and outside investors always trying to scale their business.

Setting up a Corporation

If you're setting up a corporation, then the first thing you'll need to do is register your company name and file your articles of incorporation. You'll also need to get a Federal Tax Identification Number, known as Employer Identification Number (EIN). As a corporation, you need to keep in mind that you'll have very limited liability, which means more protection for your personal assets. You'll also be able to raise your capital and sell stock to increase your chances of attracting investors. Another great thing is that you'll have to file your corporate taxes and personal taxes separately.

Setting up corporations is very difficult. The entire process can be quite long and complicated. Moreover, it requires filing out tons of paperwork and going over legalization policies that you will need to be on top of. You can also consider reaching out to a lawyer to handle this.

C Corporation

The thing about a C corporation is that the shareholders get to combine their funds to get stock in the business. The IRS regards C corporations as separate tax entities, which means they can take tax deductions. But the downside is that your earnings may get taxed twice if your income is in the form of dividends. If you want to minimize double taxation, you'll have to seek help from an experienced business accountant.

One great thing about this business structure is that it provides more protection from personal liability and amazing non-tax benefits to the owners. It allows your business to be considered a separate legal entity and has no restrictions on who can hold shares. Owners also get to enjoy well-established legal precedents that allow the seamless running of your business.

Subchapter S Corporation

The difference between an S corporation and a C corporation is that any profits or losses in an S corporation aren't taxed separately and go directly to the owners. This means that you won't have to deal with double taxation if you choose to form an S corporation because shareholders have to pay the state income tax. However, only individuals are allowed to hold stock in the business, not corporations.

If you want to become an S corporation, you'll have to register your business as a corporation first and then request for the S corporation status. Read the IRS instructions for Form 2553 to see if your company is eligible for the status or not.

B Corporation

B (Benefit) corporation is a business structure for for-profit entities, but they aren't all that different from a traditional C corporation. If you choose a B corporation instead of a non-profit, you'll still have shareholders who own the company, and the profits will return to them.

Limited Liability Corporation (LLC)

As the name suggests, LLC provides limited liability and has the flexibility of a sole proprietorship or a partnership. It's fairly new, so the benefits may vary from state to state, but it's usually very similar to an S corporation.

An LLC will be the perfect business structure for you to protect your personal assets and keep them separate from your business. It's also ideal for you if you're a part of an industry where lawsuits aren't uncommon. For comprehensive and up-to-date information on the benefits and regulations related to forming an LLC in your state, consulting local business resources and official government websites – such as the Secretary of State's office website or other relevant state agencies – is highly recommended.

Forming an LLC

To get started with forming an LLC, you'll have to pick a business name and then file your articles of organization. You also need to create an opening agreement and any permits or licenses and a DBA (stands for 'doing business as') if you need them.

As an LLC, you'll only be taxed on your share of profits, and they'll be filed on your personal taxes. In most states, you don't even need to get multiple people involved to form an LLC. It can be a great alternative to a sole proprietorship for you, depending on your business.

Partnership

A partnership, in simple terms, comprises two or more individuals that share ownership of their business. All of them get to share the profits and the losses and contribute to the business as well. Partnerships are usually governed by state laws, but a Uniform Partnership Act has now become the law in many states. According to this act, the legal core of a partnership is the agreement. The agreement defines members as either general or limited partners and mentions different levels of risk for each one.

If you decide to form a partnership, you should get in touch with an attorney with enough experience with partnerships. They'll guide you through what you need to include in the agreement and the mistakes you need to avoid.

Forming a Partnership

To form a partnership, all you need to do is run a business together with your business partner(s). But if you wish to launch a business under a name that's not yours and your partner's, then you must file a DBA, along with any licenses or permits that your particular industry requires you to file.

Before you can launch your partnership, you should know that it's better to outline an agreement in the presence of every partner's attorney to make sure you're doing it right. The perfect agreement will clearly lay out the responsibilities of each partner and any arrangements that need to be made if one of you withdraws. In a partnership, the profits and losses are passed through to all the partners. It's also advised to get a lawyer to look over your agreement.

Make sure you can trust your business partners with your credit score, your reputation, and your business before partnering up with them to avoid any problems down the road.

Following are the three types of partnerships you need to know about.

Joint venture

A joint venture is for you if you wish to partner up with someone for a particular project. These are time-specific and end after the project is completed.

General partnership

A general partnership is one where all the partners are equally involved in the business which means all the liabilities, profits, losses, and responsibilities are evenly divided.

Limited partnership

A limited partnership (LP), also known as a partnership with limited liability, is a more intricate business structure designed to accommodate partners with varying levels of involvement and responsibility. In a limited partnership, there are two types of partners: general partners and limited partners.

General partners assume full responsibility for the day-to-day operations of the business. They are actively involved in decision-making, management, and are personally liable for the company's debts and legal obligations. General partners have a direct role in steering the business and are accountable for its overall performance.

Limited partners, on the other hand, have a more passive role. Their primary contribution is financial, and they invest capital into the business without participating in its daily management. Limited partners enjoy limited liability, meaning their personal assets are typically protected from the business's liabilities. However, this protection is contingent upon them not engaging in the active management of the business.

If a limited partner starts taking an active role in the business's affairs, they may risk losing their limited liability status.

The success of a limited partnership relies on effective communication and collaboration between general and limited partners. While general partners steer the ship, limited partners provide crucial financial support, creating a symbiotic relationship that allows for a diversified approach to business management and growth. It's essential for all partners to clearly define their roles, expectations, and level of involvement from the outset to ensure the smooth functioning of the limited partnership.Top of Form

Sole Proprietorship

The easiest business structure to form is the sole proprietorship. It's a business without a separate legal entity. It's very simple to form a sole proprietorship and it's relatively low-cost, but the downside is that you can't separate your personal assets from your business assets.

It's the best form of business for you if you plan to be self-employed and want to run your small business all on your own.

Forming a Sole Proprietorship

Forming a sole proprietorship is very easy because you don't need to register your business officially. If you're selling a product you've created on an ecommerce website, then you're already a sole proprietor. However, your industry may require you to obtain any licenses or permits. And if you're doing business under a trade name and not your own, then you have to file a DBA.

The best part about being a sole proprietor is that your taxes will be relatively easy, but if you also have employees, your taxes may get a little more complicated. It may get especially difficult to get small business loans because banks don't typically see sole proprietorships as credible. You also won't be able to increase the value of your company because you can't sell any stock.

The biggest disadvantage is that if your business fails or you can't pay off your debt, your personal assets (your savings, car, house, etc.) will be in danger because you'd be assuming full liability for any legal issues that may occur.

Register Your Works

As a business, you need to protect and safeguard your intellectual property from theft, replication, or misuse by learning about copyrights, patents, and trademarks that will offer protection to your intellectual goods under the law. If you own one of these rights, then you can sue anyone who tries to use your property without your consent.

But before you can think about protecting your intellectual property, you need to figure out whether it needs to be patented, copyrighted, or trademarked.

Copyright

Copyrights protect ownership of artistic work like music, songs, poetry, novels, paintings, digital creations, etc. Copyright lasts as long as you're alive with an additional 70 years after you've passed away.

When you have legal evidence of owning your artwork, you can sue anyone who tries to misuse or replicate it in court. You should keep a record of your intellectual property to show as evidence during infringement claims.

If your work has been copyrighted, then you have the right to prevent the reproduction or copying of the works, the right to prevent the distribution or broadcasting of it to the public, and the right to prevent lending or renting it. The decision of who can use your work lies with you.

Patent

If you've invented something, like industrial processes, chemical products, commodities, equipment, etc. then you need to patent it for lawful protection. The inventor is usually the patent owner unless they give the rights to someone else. They can license it to let people use their invention or even sell it.

There are two types of patents: utility and plant patents, and design patents. Utility and plant patents can last for 20 years after you've filed the application, whereas design patents last 15 years, but you can make adjustments in the patent terms.

Your invention needs to meet certain requirements if you wish to patent them. It should be new and not have been done by anyone else before you, so try not to tell the world about your invention before you patent it. It should be a usable product instead of a theory or artwork and should serve a purpose in any industry. A patent owner reserves the right to prevent the sale, use, and import of their invention. They can also take legal action against people who've used the invention without their permission.

If you wish to acquire a patent, then you need to apply to the intellectual property office, and they will decide if your invention is patentable or not.

Trademark

A trademark is a word, phrase design, or symbol that differentiates your business and your products from similar businesses and products. Trademark rights protect your property from being used by other businesses. The most common examples of intellectual property that you may want to trademark are brand logos, names, slogans, etc. These fall under the term 'mark'. They can be registered with the patent and trademark office.

If you've registered the trademark, then you can use the ™ symbol after the mark. Once registered you can start using the ® symbol after the mark. Trademarks last as long as the mark's in use but maintenance documents are required to be filed between years 5 and 6, and 9 and 10.

To register for copyrights or patents, you need to apply to the respective intellectual property office. In the United States, the U.S. Copyright Office handles copyright registrations, and the United States Patent and Trademark Office (USPTO) manages patent registrations. For trademarks, you can also register with the USPTO. It's advisable to consult these official government offices or seek legal advice for accurate and up-to-date information on the registration processes.

Taxes Your Business Must Pay

Depending on your business activities, you need to pay different types of taxes. If you've purchased a property for your business or you're selling taxable products or services, you need to learn about the taxes that are associated with them. If you can, get a tax advisor to help you out so that you're able to understand what you need to do for your particular situation.

Income Tax

Every business is required to pay tax on their income, which is basically the profit the company makes every year. Owners of Partnerships, S corporations, and small businesses have to pay taxes through their personal income tax returns. This is called 'pass-through tax'. Sole proprietorships and LLCs owned by individuals need to pay taxes by filing a Schedule C form with their tax returns.

Self-Employment Tax

Sole proprietors and partners have to pay self-employment taxes for Medicare and Social Security, depending on their company's income. LLC owners also need to pay these taxes, but owners of corporations don't need to.

Property Tax

If you've purchased a real estate property for your business, then you must also pay a property tax to the taxing authority. This type of tax is based on your property's assessed value.

Sales Tax

Certain products and services are sales-tax eligible in some states. If you run your business in a state that has the state income tax, then you need to have a system in place to collect, report and pay the state sales tax.

Employment or Payroll Tax

These are collected like sales taxes and paid to the IRS and Social Security Administration. They are paid by owners of the business based on the gross salary of their employees. They include federal and state unemployment taxes, FICA taxes, and federal and state worker compensation taxes. Some of them, like the unemployment tax, only have to be paid by the employer.

Dividend Tax

If you're a shareholder in a corporation, then you need to pay income taxes based on the income you get from dividends.

Business Insurance

You may have dealt with many insurance policies in your life like car insurance, life insurance, health insurance, renters' insurance, and many more. The main function of insurance is to restore your property and your belongings to the state they were in before an unexpected incident occurred and damaged them, for example, you get in a car accident or your apartment gets flooded.

In the same way, businesses need insurance too so they can be protected from legal, financial, or other claims in the event of a disaster, lawsuit, accident, etc. It also safeguards your personal and business income and assets. If your business is operating without insurance then in case of a disaster or other unforeseen occurrence, you could lose all your savings and have no option but to shut down your business.

To avoid running into such problems and keep your business up and running, you need to invest in the right insurance protection for your business. But deciding which insurance policy your business needs can be quite challenging. There are several different types of business insurance and we'll discuss the most important ones in detail.

If this is an area that's too unfamiliar for you, then it's always recommended that you get an insurance agent and ask them to determine how much insurance you should get for your business depending on your business type and industry.

Workers' Compensation Insurance

If you have employees, then you may be required by law to carry workers' compensation insurance. This is needed in the event that an employee is injured or harmed on the office premises. It must not be taken lightly because your state may take legal action against you if you haven't purchased the required amount of coverage for your employees.

If any of your employees experience an injury on the job, then the workers' compensation insurance will not only cover all of their medical expenses but they'll also be paid some percentage of their wages and other health benefits as they fully recover. If your employees have received worker's compensation, then they must give up their rights to file a lawsuit against your company for any work-related injuries.

Workers' Compensation Insurance can be purchased through a private carrier or a broker. Get in touch with your state's insurance department or workers' compensation board to learn more about this.

Unemployment Insurance

This is another type of insurance that is required by the government. Unemployment insurance offers protection to your employees if they incur a job loss or get terminated. It helps them financially for a limited amount of time while they look for another job. One difference between this insurance and other types of business insurance is that it can't be purchased from an insurance carrier.

As an employer, you'll have to pay state unemployment (SUTA) and federal unemployment taxes (FUTA) among other payroll taxes. The amount of tax you have to pay depends on the number of employees working under you and whether you're an old or new business. If a person is unemployed, they can apply for unemployment benefits. This program is especially administered by the state for employers and employees.

If you're a new business owner, contact your state's unemployment agency and apply for an employer account when you're about to recruit your first ever employee. You can calculate the SUTA and FUTA and pay them by yourself, but it's advised to utilize your payroll service or HR software to get accurate calculations.

Maintain records of all your tax payments and any charges made against your unemployment insurance account by employees that no longer work for you.

Commercial Property Insurance

Commercial property insurance protects your company's equipment, office space, inventory, and other property against any loss or damage. It will pay for extensive repair and replacement expenses. As a business owner, you can select from a wide variety of property insurance policies depending on the needs of your business. There are some policies that only cover a specific cause of loss or damage like a crime policy and some only cover a specific type of damage like a fire insurance policy.

If your small business has a brick-and-mortar location, then you need to have this type of insurance. A brick-and-mortar establishment refers to a physical, tangible business location with a building or storefront, as opposed to an online or virtual business without a physical presence. Commercial property insurance provides coverage for any incidents like theft, vandalism, and even damage caused by rough weather. Most of these policies will cover flooding damage but not all of them will take care of damage caused by tornadoes and earthquakes.

To determine how much you pay for this insurance, you need to assess the value of your business assets and that includes your building. Some other factors that you'll need to consider are your location and if it's prone to natural disasters, the construction of your building and whether it was built with fireproof materials or not, if there are any fire stations nearby, etc.

You can add business interruption insurance on top of your commercial property policy to protect yourself against loss of income in case of an accident or property damage.

Business Interruption or Loss of Income Insurance

Sometimes, your company's physical property is so severely damaged that you have to stop operating your business until everything's been repaired and replaced. You may also lose the income your business could've generated during that period. That's when business interruption insurance comes into play because it's not enough to have property insurance that only covers the cost of rebuilding and replacing the damaged equipment.

Business interruption insurance helps you by providing some income to you while your property is being rebuilt. How much you get paid depends entirely on your policy. It's perfect for your business if you need financial safety and any loss of income could disrupt your business.

General Liability Insurance

General liability insurance isn't required by law, but businesses should still purchase it. It protects your business if any of your clients, customers, or vendors gets injured at your company's premises or by your products/services.

It covers the cost of any property damage to another person or business when they're handling a task for your business, any physical injuries experienced by individuals on your business property, and any advertising injury that involves slander, misappropriation, libel, etc.

It's a great coverage to have for your business if you're located in a place where accidents can easily happen or if the industry you're a part of involves serious risks —e.g. manufacturing, construction, landscaping among many others.

Employment Practices Liability Insurance

This type of insurance gives coverage to your business in case any of your employees bring up wrongful claims related to job termination or discrimination in the workplace. It would cover the cost of defending any baseless claims of racial discrimination, sexual harassment, or mistreatment of employees.

The expenses of this insurance vary depending on the size of your workforce, your industry, and whether any wrongful claims were made against your business in the past.

Even if you make efforts to keep your workplace environment fair and harmonious, you could still need EPLI. Small businesses, in particular, are at risk of wrongful termination lawsuits because they don't always have a proper HR team in place. This insurance is a must-have for them because it could save them a lot of money.

Product Liability Insurance

You need to consider product liability insurance if your business is about selling tangible goods to your customers. It can be added to your general liability insurance policy or purchased separately. The best part about this insurance policy is that it will cover all the stages that your product goes through from manufacturing to packaging. Your customers could sue you if there are any defects in the product so you need all the protection you can get from this insurance.

Key Person Insurance

This insurance policy is designed to make sure that a business can go on even after the owner dies or becomes disabled. When the owner is no longer there, the business can suffer greatly by losing income and/or clients that were brought on by the key person.

Small business owners need to purchase this type of insurance to protect their business from these types of losses. It provides a substantial payout to support the business after the owner or another important person passes away or is no longer able to perform their responsibilities anymore.

Any proceeds from this insurance can be used to hire and train a new key person for your business, to pay the salaries of your employees, to pay off any debts, etc. Determine the coverage that will be required by your business by figuring out who's your key person, how much income they help generate, and how long it could take to replace them.

Purchasing the Best Insurance for Your Small Business

As the owner of a small business, you don't have to buy all the insurances that are mentioned. Discuss your business affairs with your broker or business attorney to purchase the best types of business insurance for your company. Don't get an insurance policy if it doesn't apply to you or the chances of your business ever needing them are slim to none.

Here are some pointers you need to keep in mind to purchase the best insurance for your small business.

Do Your Research

Review the most essential business insurances and get in touch with other business owners in your industry to find out what kind of coverage is usually required for your business type. Assess different aspects of your company as well, like the property you own, the kind of natural disasters your business is prone to, and the nature of your employees.

Hire a Broker

Hire a broker so that you can get business insurance quotes that are within your budget and give your business the right amount of coverage. You can also contact insurance providers instead or even use one of the many comparison websites to compare business insurance quotes.

Ask Questions

When your broker brings in the business insurance quotes, ask questions and go over the details like coverage limited and the monthly premium. Most insurance policies for small businesses involve a deductible that has to be paid before the carrier can insure your business against any losses. Usually, if the deductible is high then that means the monthly premium will be relatively low.

Stay Updated

After you've purchased all your insurance policies, you must always make sure they're up to date. Get help from your broker if you need to. Keep relevant business insurance policies in mind when you're about to make important business decisions, because you may have to expand your coverage.

Most business insurance policies come with a one-year expiration date which means you need to renew it at the end of every year. You can even choose to switch to another insurance provider if you weren't satisfied with the old one.

One way to purchase the best insurance would be to bundle different types of insurance together in a single policy to save your business some money. If you're the owner of a home-based business, then you can simply add coverage to your homeowner's insurance policy.

Bottom Line

Running a small business involves taking risks whenever necessary to drive growth and achieve business goals. When you have your company's best interests at heart, every decision you make will advance your business.

Take all the risks into consideration and any events that might be common or uncommon in your industry to only get the protection your business needs. If you're located in an area that's vulnerable to hurricanes, then not having commercial property insurance can cost you thousands of dollars, if not more.

The unexpected can happen and your company could face the brunt of it if you're not insured. Take your time to study different types of business insurance and find the coverage that's a perfect fit for your business.

Chapter 6

The Money

Without a financial plan in place, your business won't be able to make it in the long run. It's valuable for all business owners, regardless of their business structure and how small their company is. You need to construct a business plan to be able to make important business decisions every day keeping the overall financial health and efficacy of your business in mind.

Even if you're a sole proprietor, you need to think ahead in terms of finances and make sure you'll be able to support your business in the future. The economy is ever-evolving, and you need to do everything in your capacity to make accommodations for any changes down the line.

Creating a financial plan helps you analyze future and current costs and formulate the best plan of action for your business. This plan covers every aspect of a company, from workforce training and payroll to marketing, research and development, and resource allocation.

It will also help you determine if your business is even ready to adopt newer technology or get a bigger office space. All these things need to be taken into consideration during financial planning to manage cash flow and set achievable and quantifiable goals for your business. When you take your plans of action seriously and meet all the financial obligations of your business, investors are more likely to recognize your potential and invest in your business.

Planning your finances may seem daunting if you're fairly new in the business world but you'll soon learn that it's the best thing you can do for your small business.

Determine Financial Needs

As a new business owner, you need to make sure you have enough cash to help your business survive the first couple of months. It may take a long time for your sales revenue to start keeping up with your costs. You need to realize that losses are completely natural in the beginning, and it can stay that way for at least a year before you can expect to make any sizable profit.

During those days, you'll need to evaluate your business's financial needs to ensure you have adequate funds.

Expenses

The first thing you need to do is estimate your expenses. They can be categorized into one-time costs and recurring expenses. One-time startup costs can include office equipment and supplies, real estate, consulting services, product design, license or permit fees, etc. Recurring expenses are rent or lease payments, materials needed for production, marketing costs, financing costs, salaries, and more, depending on the industry.

After determining your expenses, you need to determine the working and starting capital you need to ensure the smooth operation of all your business processes.

Financial Resources

To kick start your entrepreneurial journey, you'll need to secure financial resources. There are various avenues you can secure your funding from. Some common resources to get funding for your startup are as follows:

Personal investment

As an entrepreneur, you're the first person who's required to invest in your business. You may have to use your savings or your personal assets as collateral to finance your business.

Debt Financing

There are several types of debt financing like lines of credit and term loans that can be tapped into to support your small business. There are lenders who offer loans specifically to startups and have flexible terms of repayment.

Individuals seeking to learn about various forms of debt financing can access several different resources. Many online platforms offer financial courses and financial websites also provide comprehensive guides. Local workshops, professional networks, and government resources also serve as valuable educational avenues. For example, in the United States, the Small Business Administration (SBA) offers resources and workshops on financing options for small businesses. Consulting with financial advisors or attending seminars at academic institutions can also further aid understanding. By leveraging these resources, individuals can make informed decisions regarding debt financing tailored to their needs and circumstances.

Friends and Family

If your friends and family support your business idea as much as you do, then they can also provide capital for your business. This is also known as 'love money'. This form of funding can offer initial support when traditional financing options may be challenging. It's crucial to approach these arrangements professionally, clearly outlining terms and expectations to avoid potential strain on personal relationships.

For example, imagine you're starting a boutique bakery, and your cousin is passionate about your venture. They may choose to invest in your business by giving you the much-needed capital for equipment or initial inventory.

Outside Equity Financing

Venture capital funds, angel investors, or business incubators can also provide funds if they see high growth potential in your business. These third parties may take an equity position in your company in exchange for their funds.

Venture capital funds are basically investment funds that are made up of contributions from wealthy companies or individuals, angel investors are individuals who provide capital for startups at the early stages, and business incubators are companies that help new businesses grow by providing services like office space and management training.

Create a Budget

Creating a budget for your business is necessary to make it more efficient, stay out of debt, estimate how long it will take to become profitable, and see a little bit into the future of your company. It can also help you ensure long-term success and allow you to spend money on the right resources at the right time.

Sales Revenue

Before deciding on a budget, set some sales goals to figure out how much you expect to make. This will allow you to determine the number of units you'll need to produce and the number of clients you'll need to cater to.

Here are a few things to consider that can help you determine how much revenue you can expect to make:

1. **Define Your Objectives:** Clearly outline your sales objectives. These could include targets for monthly, quarterly, or annual revenue, as well as the number of units sold or clients served.
2. **Consider Market Factors:** Analyze market trends, customer demand, and competitive landscape to set realistic and achievable sales goals. Understanding your industry's benchmarks can provide valuable insights.
3. **Account for Growth:** If your business is in a growth phase, factor in potential expansion and increased market share. Adjust your goals to align with the scalability of your operations.

As an example, suppose you are launching an e-commerce store selling handmade jewelry. Through market research, you identify a niche demand for unique, artisanal pieces. You estimate that, based on your pricing strategy, you can sell 200 pieces per month at an average price of $50 each. This translates to an expected monthly revenue of $10,000.

Production Cost

Then you need to think about the number of products or services you'll have to sell to meet your sales goals. This will help you determine production costs and you'll be able to see if your revenue goals are achievable or not based on that.

Operating Expenses

Calculate your operating expenses. They will vary from industry to industry and include salaries, office-related expenses, and marketing and sales expenses like advertising costs.

Cash

Calculate how much cash you have and have an estimate of how much you can spend on your business. Also, figure out how much you'll need in the future. Cash flow statements will let you see where all your money is being spent and allow you to set some aside for short-term liabilities.

Emergencies

When creating a budget, you need to be mindful of emergencies. Emergency funds will help you stabilize your business in the event where you experience major property damage due to a storm and your insurance policy doesn't cover everything. It's kept in the category of retained earnings on your balance sheet. Retained earnings are basically revenue that's left after all the liabilities and expenses have been taken care of.

Establish a Business Accounting System

It's important to have an accounting system in place to see if your company is making a profit. As an owner of a small business, it will allow you to check your sources of income and expenses and make informed business decisions. You need to use accounting software to be able to generate reports on cash flow, profit and loss, undeposited funds, aged receivables, sales register, and bank register to gauge an idea about your company's success in terms of finances.

You can choose between two accounting methods: Cash basis accounting and accrual accounting.

Cash Basis Accounting

This type of accounting is commonly used by small businesses as it allows you to record new income right as it's received and your expenses are recorded when you pay, not when you're billed.

Accrual Accounting

The Accrual system, on the other hand, is where both your income and expenses are recorded as they're earned or billed. It shows a more honest picture of your company's progress each month, but it's more difficult to manage for small businesses.

CASH	ACCRUAL
Revenue is recorded when cash is received	Revenue is recorded when it is earned
Expenses are recorded when cash is spent	Expenses are recorded when they are incurred
Income is taxed only when cash has been received	Income is taxed even if cash has not been received

Cash Basis Accounting vs. Accrual Accounting
https://old.ageras.com/blog/accrual-accounting-vs-cash-basis-accounting]

There are many widely available accounting tools and software that can help you keep your accounting, tax, and bookkeeping information in sync. You can even opt for free tools if your business can't afford the added expenditure.

Just like anything else, make sure you choose the correct accounting system, and that your chosen system is working perfectly fine because even the smallest mistake can set you back a few days. If none of your team members is an expert at accounting, then you need to consider outsourcing your accounting process or hiring a trustworthy accountant for your business. You may also want to consider meeting with a financial advisor to help you out.

Accounting systems aren't just valuable for creating financial reports and calculating your taxes, they have a great deal of information about your business that you can use to make better judgments about your business growth.

Establish a Business Bank Account

It's necessary for you to have a business bank account to handle your expenses and taxes easily. As a business owner, you'll be able to plan your budget, process payments, manage cash flow, and generate financial reports to show your investors or business partners. It also makes bookkeeping less of a hassle.

There are different types of business bank accounts that you can set up depending on your business affairs, but it's always better to ask your accountant for advice regarding this matter. Some common business accounts include savings, checking, and credit card accounts.

Do your research and then select a bank with the best services for your small business. Don't just open a business account at the same place as your personal account. There are banks made specifically for different industries, and their banking offers and benefits may be a better fit for your business needs.

Some factors you need to consider before choosing a bank are as follows:

- Early termination fees (if you wish to end a bank contract)
- Transaction fees

- Introductory bonuses
- Interest rates for business line of credit
- Interest rates for savings and checking accounts
- Monthly fees waived if you maintain a minimum balance

But before you can approach the bank and open an account, you need to contact them to ask about the paperwork you'll have to submit. You'll be expected to at least provide the following items:

- Business license or paperwork detailing business name registration
- Proof of incorporation (for business structures such as LLCs)
- Social security number (for a sole proprietary)
- Employer Identification Number (EIN) (you can get it from the IRS free of cost)

To make sure your company can also accept payments, you'll need to set up a merchant services account that allows you to receive payments. Before deciding on an account, make sure it meets the following criteria:

- Transaction fees
- Discount rates (percentage charged per transaction)
- Address verification service fees (to prevent fraud)
- Minimum monthly fees
- Low ACH (Automated Clearing House) daily batch fees to settle daily credit card transactions. In the context of credit card transactions, ACH is used to process the settlement of funds between the merchant (business) and the acquiring bank.

If your business accepts online payment, then check out online payment systems like PayPal or Stripe.

You Need a D-U-N-S

We all know that a business will eventually require a line of credit, which is why you need a DUNS (or Data Universal Numbering System) number as well!

Business owners generally hire the services of a lawyer to attain articles of incorporation and secure their financial tax ID numbers. This helps in starting the company without any hiccups. However, once you get to running this company, you will soon realize that the startup capital sitting in your bank isn't necessarily enough, particularly due to cash flow fluctuations.

This is where your DUNS number will step in to save the day.

You will need a DUNS number to get a line of credit and ensure smooth business operations. And no, it isn't the same as a federal tax ID number.

Think of it this way; you have your personal credit score, which helps you secure personal loans, right? Similarly, the DUNS number is related to your business credit, which helps potential lenders gauge your business' financial standing and reputation. The DUNS number basically determines the creditworthiness of your business.

Reports have shown that 43% of small businesses apply for loans annually. Of these, 36% are either completely or partially rejected due to their low credit scores. To make matters worse, over 29% of small businesses fail each year as they run out of capital.

Needless to say, having a solid business line of credit can help you through such times of crisis. It is also a great way to ensure more profitable terms with your vendors, lenders, and suppliers. You can achieve all this and much more through your DUNS number.

Your DUNS is a 9-digit number issued by Dun & Bradstreet, a data analytics services provider. It is a unique number assigned to a business that helps in identifying its business credit file. When you get a DUNS, your business becomes a part of a massive database with 225 million other companies.

Using the DUNS, lenders, investors, and potential business partners can get better insights into the financial stability and reliability of your business. On the other hand, business owners can look up the

DUNS number of other companies to conduct competitive analysis and determine whether they should form partnerships.

Get a Business Line of Credit

Sometimes, to grow as a business, you need to have access to working capital. When your business experiences cash flow uncertainty, then dipping into funds can definitely help you stay on track, at least for the time being. There are a ton of options to consider when it comes to business financing but getting a business line of credit seems to be the right choice for most small businesses.

To put it simply, a line of credit is a predetermined amount of funds that you can borrow to make business purchases and pay back later. Don't mistake it for a term loan because you can pay it back anytime and there are no early repayment fees. Lines of credit are also always available because after you've repaid the amount, you can use it again if the need arises. Term loans, however, are used only once and repaid with interest.

When you have a line of credit for your business, you can handle your most important operations without having to wait for your clients to pay their invoices. A credit line can help you with the following:

- Getting a new office space or expanding to different locations
- Recruiting new employees to meet increasing demands
- Purchasing new equipment or extra inventory to prepare for the holiday season

It can also be used to manage cash flow when your sales aren't doing so well, and you need to pay your employees their salaries. It can be a huge source of ease for you especially when you're going through challenges in the early stages of your business. If you can deal with business credit cards, then they should also be fairly simple to use.

Secured and Unsecured Business Credit Card

A business credit card is needed to finance your business as it allows you to cover initial and ongoing costs and they have higher limits than personal credit cards. Before you can apply for it, you need to make sure you have good personal and business credit scores so that the creditor can approve your corporation for an account.

Your business may not have a credit rating. In that case, opening a business credit card will create a new business credit file under your company's name. Aside from all the paperwork, you'll have to submit, the creditor may also ask for more information about your business, for example, the number of years you've spent in business, your industry, and what you plan to do with the business credit card. You may also be asked to reveal your personal income, where you live if you're married, and how many children you have as well. You can request more cards for your employees. If your card issuers allow, you can also design the cards with your business logo.

When you apply for a business credit card, your business credit and your personal credit will play a role. You may have to consider applying for a secured business card if your credit history doesn't fulfill the requirements for an unsecured business credit card.

A secured credit card will require you to make a security deposit when you're signing up so that the lender can mitigate risk. This deposit is either less than or equal to your credit limit. If you're able to make all your payments on time, you'll be able to get your deposit back. This type of credit card is a good option for business owners who need to rebuild credit.

Unsecured business credit cards, on the other hand, don't require a deposit. You'll have a credit limit, and you can spend up to that limit, and then pay back the balance. These business credit cards come with a variety of options, so you have the option to select a card that gives you the best rewards for your spending.

Payment Gateway Selection

If you're the owner of an online business that requires you to set up an ecommerce website, then you need to pick the right payment gateway that suits your business. There are three key players involved in any online transaction: the business owner, the customer, and the technology that connects the two.

As the business owner, you are the merchant, and you have to partner with a payment gateway that will accept any payments for you and deposit them into your account. The customer has to buy the service or product they're interested in, so they'll need a debit or credit card for that purpose. The issuing bank will provide them with the cash they need to pay you. The technology is where payment gateway and payment processor come into play.

The payment gateway is software that connects the buyer's shopping card to the network that processes payments. The payment processor does all the dirty work like moving the transaction through the network, interacting with the bank, sending a billing statement, etc.

To select the right payment gateway, you need to ask the following questions:

- Does your preferred gateway support your business type?
- Is it globally accepted?
- What's the customer experience like? Does it provide live technical support?
- What are the fees?
- Will it work in the future too?

After you've answered these questions, you can select the best payment gateway and integrate it into your website to make it easier for your customers to make payments.

Bottom Line

Financial planning is crucial for any business because sometimes the only reason your business isn't able to achieve success is that it lacks a comprehensive and effective financial plan. There's nothing wrong with getting help from a financial advisor. They'll help you formulate the best plan of action keeping your business requirements and financial situation in mind to help your business become stable and profitable.

If your business isn't making any progress, then cutting overhead costs is the first step you need to take to minimize losses and steer your company back to stability. Some ways you can manage your overhead costs are by hiring an accountant who'll effectively handle your finances if it's not your strongest suit.

Go paperless if you can and prioritize your business needs to ensure you're spending wisely. Location is another crucial element that most businesses don't pay attention to. Make sure your company is located in an area that's affordable and where rental prices won't make managing cash flow difficult for you down the road.

With the right financial plan, you can be confident that you will reach all your business goals within the expected time.

Chapter 7

Team Worthy

One of the most important and challenging tasks of building a company from scratch is picking a winning team. When you're fairly new to entrepreneurship, you need all hands on deck to get your business off the ground. Without a good team by your side, it's harder to turn your business idea into a reality.

To build a competent team, you need to recruit individuals who are driven, experienced, talented, and passionate about their work. Their personalities should fit nicely within your organization, and each member should play a significant role in driving your company forward.

During the recruitment process, you should look for people whose values align with your company's values the most. Use your cultural statement to help accomplish this; it will also help weed out candidates. This way, you'll be able to pick the right members to form a cohesive team.

It's not always necessary that a candidate who looks great on paper will prove beneficial for your company. Sometimes, an individual with little to no experience may be a dark horse. There's no one-size-fits-all formula, that's why recruitment is the trickiest aspect of building a company. There's no way to know who could turn out to be a valuable asset and who could hold your company back.

But there are some characteristics to take note of and some red flags to watch out for during talent acquisition. The next two sections in the book will walk you through what to look for in a candidate and the red flags to avoid. It's also important to consider what kind of people will be perfect for different industries and job responsibilities. If you're looking to hire a graphic designer, then you won't be looking for the same qualities as you would if you were to hire a research analyst.

Different roles require individuals with different skills. A content writer doesn't need to have strong interpersonal skills, but an HR executive does. You need to find people that would fit their role exceptionally well and you need people with great judgment skills to handle the recruitment process for you.

Building a team isn't just about finding people that will help you achieve your goals. You need team members that will add value to your organization and will be able to withstand all kinds of pressure as your company grows and evolves.

For example, in its early days, the Walt Disney Company was known for its animated work. Walt Disney, himself an animator, hired top animators because that was what the company was known for. He also hired top storytellers and innovators who understood the goal he was working towards and walked alongside him on the same path.

As one of the largest brands in the world today, Disney's success can be attributed to the people that brought it forward, rather than just the person who started the business.

What to Look for When You're Hiring

Humility

Humility is the most underrated quality of humans. What most people don't realize is that so many times, the one thing that keeps people from working together harmoniously is their ego and pride. When an individual is humble, they're more likely to take responsibility for their actions and put the company's goals above everything else.

These types of people are a lot easier to manage as well because there are fewer chances of internal conflicts. When you're starting out as a small business, any discord amongst your team members doesn't bode well for you. You need a group of people that have common goals and no selfish motives of their own. If they put your company first and are aware of what's expected of them, they'll do what it takes to take your company to success.

Confidence and Self-Awareness

You need to search for people who are confident in their skills and abilities and can hold their own under pressure. They shouldn't be afraid of new challenges. Their 'can do' attitude will take your business through the toughest of times safely and their belief in themselves will create a culture that's conducive to growth and new opportunities. These people will question your business practices constructively and that will keep you from making mistakes that could put your company at risk.

Your team members also need to be self-aware enough to know what lies outside their capabilities and what they can undertake. An individual who doesn't know their strengths and weaknesses won't say no to work that may be well outside their level of expertise, not only wasting your time but also potentially putting your company in danger.

You need to recruit candidates who know who they are and wish to make their way up in their careers. They'll have more to offer your company than just what they've been assigned because they'll be actively looking for opportunities to prove themselves.

People Who Are in It for More Than a Paycheck

When your team members are only interested in getting a paycheck at the end of the day, then that says a lot about the amount of work they'll be putting in. When you're fresh in the business world and you're pulling out all the stops to gain a foothold in your industry, you need to have people on your side that care about your business as much as you do.

If your team members are focused on reaching the targets you've set for your business, they'll come in each day with an open mind and a problem-solving attitude because they want to make significant contributions toward your company's success. People who are only interested in what they can get out of your company will only stay with you as long as it benefits them.

As a startup, you need people that will commit to your business and their determination alone will help carry your business forward.

Adaptability

When you're building a team, you need to think long-term because there are people who'll be the perfect fit for your company in the early stages, but as soon as you start evolving and expanding, these people will have a hard time adapting to the changing needs of the organization. You want people who'll perform well no matter where you stand as an organization.

During the early days, people with a spirit for new beginnings will be great at laying the foundation and coming up with new ideas to drive your company to greater heights. But in the growth mode, the same people should learn how to embrace processes and make active efforts to adapt to the systems in place. Innovative thinking is great when your company needs all the recognition it can get, but once you've been established as a credible business, giving your employees the same kind of freedom will work against you.

Integrity

You need to recruit people with a strong moral compass. Employees who take their actions seriously and wish to do the right thing regardless of what they may or may not be getting out of it will also be loyal to your organization. They'll keep private information confidential, they'll respect your company's policies, and they won't misuse any equipment they've been provided. They will also be more likely to learn from their mistakes and take full responsibility for them. Their honesty and integrity will make them a dependable asset for your company because they'll give you no reason to mistrust them. You don't want employees who don't care if they're bending or breaking rules and covering up mistakes every chance they get.

It's difficult to learn about someone's personal code of conduct because everyone's on their best behavior during the recruitment process. Asking the right questions can help you dig deeper and find the candidate you've been looking for. Ask them about their past failures and what they did to get over them. Only people who are able to admit failure will come up with a good response to this and that's how you'll know if they're perfect for your team.

Red Flags to Watch out for in Candidates

Candidates That Don't Ask Questions

When you're faced with a candidate that doesn't ask any questions about your company's vision and long-term growth plans, you need to be especially wary of them. People who don't seem interested are usually just looking for a job to either kill time or figure out what they actually want to do in life. Your organization could just be a temporary place for them until they find the right career path.

As the owner of a small business that's only just starting out, you want to stay away from these people because it takes time, resources, and money to go through the recruitment process all over again. That's why you need to hire people who show interest every step of the way and ask you about where your company is headed and what you wish to achieve in the future.

Candidates That Haven't Done Their Research

There's nothing worse than taking your time out to interview people only to find out they don't know the most basic things about your company. When you're investing the effort to learn about the candidate beforehand, you can expect to be greeted with the same level of commitment. When someone has an idea about your company and what it stands for, it shows that they take their work seriously.

You need candidates that will support your business in the early stages, not people who just want something to do while they look for better opportunities. Their lack of preparation can be an indication of their work ethic down the line. If they can't even bother to read up before coming in for an interview, then there's no reason for you to believe they won't bring the same attitude to work once they're hired.

Candidates That Badmouth Former Employers

When candidates are too honest in the interview, they'll open up about their past employment experiences and talk about any grudges they have against their former employers. This should ring alarm bells because it shows a clear lack of professionalism on their end. It just goes to show that they're likely to cast everything in a negative light that doesn't happen according to their expectations.

You shouldn't take their word for it either because it could simply be a misunderstanding or their own mistake that they don't want to own up to. You need to realize that if they can talk behind someone else's back in an interview then nothing would keep them from badmouthing you to other people.

Keeping a Winning Team

You can hire the best people for your team who will exceed all your expectations in terms of performance, but you shouldn't forget that providing them with an environment where their needs are recognized and met is just as important. After your company gets beyond the initial stages, you need to make sure your team is doing better than ever at adapting because you can't risk losing them after you've trained them through the worst days.

You need to keep them satisfied and provide them with ample opportunities to prove their expertise. Even the most skilled and talented individuals can get affected if the culture of your organization doesn't improve as your company evolves. You need to lead your employees by example if you want to keep them around for long. Take accountability for your actions as a leader and be honest about your business practices.

Inspire your team every day by maintaining honest communication with them and showing compassion whenever necessary. If they feel like they belong and are appreciated when they help the company reach a milestone, they'll do even better. You can't have a great team if you're not willing to sacrifice your time and effort into building and managing it.

You also need to make sure you've given appropriate office space to all your teams because their work may require a more open setting, especially if they're in the design team. Do your research about what works for people in different departments and make sure everyone is comfortable with the arrangement because something as simple as low lighting can have an adverse effect on someone's performance.

Bottom Line

Even after you've spent time and money building the perfect team for your company, you need to understand that there truly is no such thing as the perfect team or the perfect manager. It all depends on how everyone works together and brings out the best in each other.

Managers have their work cut out for them because they'll be held responsible if their team's performance is subpar. They should know when to step in and guide their team through the trickiest of times and make sure no one is left behind.

It will take time to find the right balance and understand where everyone fits in the organization before you can expect to make any headway. Don't take your employees for granted and appreciate their efforts every chance you get to evoke their sense of belonging.

Chapter 8

Brand Marketing

Marketing is a form of communication that's used to promote your products and services and convince people to buy them. It's the process of letting your target audience know that what you have to offer is everything they've been looking for. It's an all-encompassing procedure that involves all the stages of getting your product or service to the consumer.

When you're creating a marketing plan, you need to keep in mind that it should:

- Capture the attention of your target market
- Persuade consumers to purchase your product or service
- Provide the customers with the easiest action they can take to receive your product or service

The buyer personas that you've developed can be used as a guide when you're formulating your marketing strategies. They will allow you to produce content and create messaging that would attract your target customers. You can personalize your marketing for different customer segments as well.

Marketing helps you reach your business goals. It's meant to increase sales and make new customers for your business. There are several marketing channels that can be used to market your business —social media, email marketing, content marketing, and SEO, word-of-mouth marketing, etc.

Social Media

Social media has a huge influence on the business world because most of the world has an online presence and it's easier to reach them now more than ever. Customers are looking for brands on social media channels to see what they're like before making the purchase.

It's great for small businesses in particular because they can take full advantage of it and reach a large number of people spending little to no money. It provides them with community-building opportunities allowing them to promote their brand mission and story.

Here's what you need to consider leveraging this platform for all it's worth.

Be Transparent

It's important to let your followers or prospective customers in on what goes on behind the scenes at your company. Post content that will give them an insight into your business processes and address any complaints in the comment section gracefully. When you're open and honest with your customers, they're more likely to trust you and buy your products and services.

Build Relationships

Your primary goal on a social media channel shouldn't be to increase sales and gain more customers. Instead, you should focus on building strong and loyal relationships with your customers first because retaining customers is the only way you can expect to be successful in the long run. Consumers would go to your website to buy products, not your social media profile. They come here to find out about your business and see if you look credible as a brand. Try to post engaging content to grab their attention right away and respond to their queries in a way that makes them feel special and prioritized.

Choose the Right Platforms

Use your research about your customers to figure out which platforms they use more frequently. It is important to know that all platforms aren't beneficial to all businesses. For example, a store will benefit from Facebook and Pinterest while a law firm will benefit from LinkedIn and Twitter. This way, you'll know where to be more active and consistent with your content and where you can lay low, at least at the beginning.

Content Marketing and SEO

Content marketing is creating valuable and relevant content to engage your audience and get them to do what you want them to do. SEO, also known as Search Engine Optimization, is a technical process that's focused on getting more traffic to your website. It involves making changes to your content and website design to make it more attractive for search engines.

If you want your content to rank higher in the search results, you need to incorporate the right keywords and phrases. These are queries that are typed in by users when they're looking for solutions to a problem they're facing or when they're looking for something specific.

To get the most out of content marketing, you need to:

Have a Plan in Mind

You need to have a strategy in mind before creating and publishing your content. Using your buyer personas and value proposition about your audience's challenges and pain points and try to write about them to catch their eye. You can also have a call-to-action in your content to get your readers to try your products or get in contact with you.

Make Valuable Content

Your content needs to serve a purpose, so it should be valuable. Include imagery and videos wherever you can to make it interesting to read. The introduction should be tempting enough to get people to continue reading your blog or article.

Distribute It across Multiple Channels

It's not enough to publish all your content on your website. You need to distribute it across different channels like social media pages or guest posting on other sites. You should direct people to your website by adding links where necessary.

Word-Of-Mouth Marketing

No matter how fast the world is progressing, word-of-mouth marketing is still one of the most effective ways of marketing. When customers are told by people, they trust to try out a product, they're more likely to act on it as opposed to a salesperson telling them the same thing.

Some ways to encourage word-of-mouth marketing are as follows:

Reputation Management

Whenever a customer purchases a product or service, reach out to them, ask them for their feedback, and give them an option to leave a review as well. Ask your loyal customers directly to write it for you. Add these reviews on your website as testimonials to let prospective customers know that your products and services have been tried and approved by other people.

Referral or Affiliate Programs

Ask your customers to refer other people like their friends and family members to you and offer them an incentive like a discount or credit every time their referrals get in touch with you for your products or services.

Email Marketing

Email marketing is the use of emails to build relationships with prospective customers. It's a method of direct response marketing. Users that have provided you their contact information want to hear from you. This doesn't mean you should spam everyone with your deals every chance you get.

You should include valuable information in your emails about your products or services and how people can benefit from them to make your customers take notice of them.

Some of the best practices of email marketing include:

Keep Them Short

No one has the time to read long emails. Keep your email brief and to the point. Make them easy to read and get through. Add a call-to-action at the bottom.

Personalize

Use what you've learned about your customers and personalize the emails. A simple yet effective way to personalize is by using the customer's name in the email greeting. Utilize segmentation practices to send relevant emails to all your receivers. For example, imagine you run an online clothing store that caters to various demographics. Through segmentation, you can categorize your customers based on factors such as purchase history, location, or preferences. Then, you can send targeted emails featuring products or promotions specifically relevant to each segment. For instance, if you have a segment of customers interested in winter wear, tailor emails showcasing new winter arrivals to those customers.

Add a Tempting Subject Line

The subject line plays a crucial role in encouraging recipients to open your email, but it's essential to strike the right balance to avoid sounding spammy or like a hacker. Overly aggressive or misleading subject lines, such as "You've Won a Prize, Click Here Now!" or "Urgent Action Required: Your Account Is Compromised," can often trigger spam filters or raise suspicions among recipients. Keep the subject line concise yet compelling, aiming to provide genuine value or an enticing incentive. Consider incorporating elements that grab attention without appearing overly promotional. By maintaining authenticity and relevance, you'll not only increase the likelihood of your emails being opened but also foster trust with your audience. Remember, a well-crafted subject line should spark curiosity rather than raise suspicions.

Pay-Per-Click Advertising

Even with so many diverse marketing techniques out there, Pay-Per-Click advertising still works just as well, if not better. Use Google Ads or Social media ads like Instagram/Facebook ads to connect with your target customers. It's a way to let people know of your presence and introduce them to your products and services.

Bottom Line

The brand is bigger than marketing because marketing can only contribute to it. The brand, however, is everything that comes to mind when you think about a business. Marketing will help you get the word out about your brand, but your brand is a stand-alone concept that gives your business an identity.

While marketing attracts customers and allows you to actively increase sales, branding focuses on building strong and loyal customer relationships for long-term success. Still, needless to say, a brand without a good marketing plan won't gain any traction, and a marketing strategy without a solid brand to promote will have no substance or appeal.

How you choose to market your products and services may differ because what will and won't work depends entirely on your business. The secret to success in marketing is creating a brand, formulating a plan, sticking to it, and using the time and resources necessary to achieve your goals.

Chapter 9

Revenue, Business Model & Business Plan

Your business won't become successful overnight. It takes time, effort, and money spent intelligently to get to a place where you can expect to achieve greatness. When you're first starting out, the only thing you have is a concept of what your business is about and the product or service you're going to sell to people. There are no clear objectives and only the faintest idea of where you wish to be within the next few years.

But when you have a whole team working under you and customers to cater to, not having a plan simply won't do. How can your business become profitable if you haven't laid out clear business objectives and formulated any strategies to achieve them?

To make sure your business reaches all the targets you've set and more, you need to have a well-defined business plan, revenue and business model. They all serve different purposes and are constructed quite differently too.

As a business owner, you need to know the key differences between the three to understand how your business can benefit from all of them.

A business model is basically the mechanism that allows your company to make a profit. It's a document that delineates your company's relationship with suppliers, clients, and key partners. It also defines the key resources needed for your business to prosper, the cost structure, and other such aspects that set your business apart from the rest.

A revenue model is a part of your overall business model. It aims to explain the different mechanisms your business will employ to generate a stable income. The business model lists down these mechanisms, their sources, and other effective ways to make money for your business based on what is offered and the entity that pays for it.

A business plan is simply a blueprint that details the core aspects of your business. It serves as a prospectus that you can show any potential investors to give them an idea about your company's business strategies and what they can expect from it in the future. It's a document that describes all the core functionalities of your business in the most presentable way.

They hold equal importance, are living documents, and need to be prepared with extreme forethought, but you must know there isn't one right way of doing it. It's all about coming up with a plan that fits your business perfectly. What works for you might not work for other businesses and vice versa.

Revenue Model

Deciding how your business will generate a steady stream of revenue is one of the essential, yet most challenging aspects of running a company. You might know exactly what goods or services you're going to sell. But, how will you ensure that people buy them?

Your revenue has to be sufficient enough to account for any manufacturing costs, salaries, office running expenses, etc. Moreover, the lack of a well-defined revenue model can result in your business only making enough money to match its expenses, without ever earning you a profit.

Your revenue model looks into all of these factors and helps you create a sustainable strategy that fits whatever you're trying to sell. It dictates how a business should charge its customers for the goods or services being offered, ensuring that it is sufficient to make up for expenses while also allowing you a certain percentage of profit. These models highlight the most effective ways of making money specifically for your business, based on what you're offering and who will be paying for it.

There are numerous types of revenue models you can consider for your business:

- **Advertising Revenue Model**

If you sell an advertising space to generate money, you're using an advertising revenue model. This works if the seller has a sought after space for advertising that offers high customer traffic and visibility, either in real life or in the digital world.

- **Affiliate Revenue Model**

Businesses that use affiliate revenue models generate their income through commissions. These business sell items belonging to other retailers and earn a percentage of the sale for themselves.

- **Freemium Revenue Model**

The Freemiun revenue model allows a company to offer its customers a basic or limited service for free. Users are given access to certain features of a service at no cost, but required to pay a premium for any advanced or extra features.

- **Recurring Revenue Model**

Also called the subscription model, these plan out revenue generation by charging customers at regular time intervals. These can be monthly, quarterly, yearly etc.

- **Sales Revenue Model**

Sales Revenue Models allow you to generate income by selling goods or services either in person or online. So, any business that directly sells to its customers should utilize the sales revenue model.

- **SaaS Revenue Model**

SaaS stands for Software as a Service, and this revenue model allows customers to be charged on an interval basis for a software that they may be using. These businesses are often focused on customer retention and have a subscription pricing model.

Business Model

A business model is important because it encompasses all the foundational assumptions about your business and provides a framework for success. It shows how your company will create value and overcome any challenges in the future. It simply paints a clear picture of where your business is headed and what you need to do to take it there.

It consists of the following items:

- Customer Segments
- Value Proposition
- Channels
- Customer Relationships
- Revenue Streams
- Key Resources
- Key Activities
- Key Partners
- Cost Structures

Customer Segments

When you're creating your business model, you need to break down your customer segment into two or three comprehensive buyer's personas based on their age, gender, interests, and purchasing habits. Layout their specifics, the common challenges they face in everyday life, and how your company will solve them. We went over this in chapter 2.

Value Proposition

Your value proposition is what makes you stand out from your competitors. You need to state exactly what your business is here to offer and why it's better than the rest. A good value proposition shows how you'll add value to your customers' lives. Use your research from chapter 2.

Channels

Channels are entities that you'll have to use to spread the word about your business and reach your target market. Channels are also used to sell your products and provide your services to the customers. They include social media channels, emails, networking, viral marketing, affiliates, etc. Reference what you learned in chapter 8.

Customer Relationships

How your business interacts with its customers is termed as customer relationship. Some examples of this can be in-person communication, online communication, at events, or through third-party contractors.

Revenue Streams

The revenue stream is the process that converts your value proposition into financial gain for your business. You need to choose a revenue model that suits your company perfectly. Here are some examples of revenue models you can choose:

1. **Pay-Per-Product:** Earn revenue by charging customers a specific amount for each product or unit sold, ensuring direct correlation between sales and income.
2. **Fee for Service:** Generate revenue by charging fees for specific services provided, offering a straightforward and transparent pricing structure.
3. **Subscription:** Establish a recurring revenue stream by offering subscription-based services, where customers pay regularly for ongoing access to your products or content.
4. **Freemium:** Combine free and premium offerings, attracting a broader audience with basic services while generating revenue through premium features or upgrades.
5. **Equity Gain:** Generate revenue through equity ownership, often associated with startups where investors gain returns as the company's valuation increases.

Key Resources

These are the main resources that your business needs to survive. They include office space, computers, staff, internet, electricity, and transport among many other things.

Key Activities

Key activities are the actions you need to take to provide value to your customers in the form of products or services. They can be anything from designing, web development, and content creation to driving and baking.

Key Partners

Key partners are suppliers, alliances, or other external companies that help you run your company. These are entities that your business can't exist without.

Cost Structures

The cost structure of your business is the total financial cost you need to operate your business. It includes the cost it will take to achieve your company's key activities, obtain and utilize your key resources, gain access to your key partners as well as other additional costs.

Business Plan

This is where all the research you've done for your business comes in handy. Before you can prepare a business plan, you need to think critically about the most common challenges a small business can face in your industry. What you've learned about your competitors and their business practices should help you come up with effective business strategies for your company.

Your business plan should have everything that your company stands for and hopes to achieve because it will help you make important business decisions in the future. It should clearly define your company's position in the marketplace by describing your products/services, your prospective customers, how you can reach them, and what you need to do to become successful.

The perfect business plan will guide you through all the phases of your business and give you a sense of direction.

Here's what a business plan usually involves:

- Executive Summary
- Business Description
- Market Analysis
- Management Plan
- Operations Plan
- Critical Risks
- Financial Projections
- Appendices

Executive Summary

An executive summary gives an overview of your business plan, that's why it's typically written at the end. It's called a summary because it briefly goes over the key points discussed in the document so that the readers know what to expect. It needs to state everything in clear terms and describe the content of the document concisely. But it should also be interesting enough to make the readers turn the page and read the rest of the plan.

It's the most important part of a business plan because this is where you can make a great first impression on your reader. If you're showing it to potential investors or banks, then it should catch their attention right away.

As the owner of a small business, one of the main goals of writing a business plan is to convince angel investors, venture capitalists, or banks to invest in your business. An executive summary for a startup usually summarizes the following:

- The business opportunity that describes the need for your business
- How you plan to take advantage of it and serve the market
- The customers you'll be targeting
- Your business model
- Your marketing plans for your products or services
- Your competitors and your strategy for getting market share and what makes you different from them
- Your financial plan
- All the members and the role they play in your business
- Your implementation plan

Business Description

A business description explains the key aspects of your business and provides the scope of your business idea. When investors and lenders read your business description, they should immediately see the need for your business in the marketplace and how it will benefit the customers. As your business grows and expands, you need to update your business description as well.

The most common elements of a business description include the company name, the type of business structure, names of all the owners or partners, the location, the company history, the mission statement, the products/services being offered, the target customers, the business objectives and the future of the company.

Your business description should have all the vital information about your business and it should accurately reflect the passion that led you to start your business. Try to get the point across in as few words as possible and make sure the information you've added isn't redundant and distracting.

Market Analysis

The market analysis section of the business plan gives detailed information about the industry you'll be selling your products/services in, your target market and competitors, and how you'll make a place for your business in the market.

It should also have detailed statistics about the industry size, growth rate and trends, and the demographics of your target customers like age, gender, income bracket, and lifestyle preferences. You also need to include the results of any market research you conducted to investigate the industry.

It's important to conduct comprehensive market research beforehand to make sure your business plan appears credible. Try to look at the industry through the eyes of a consumer to pinpoint the problems and how your business can solve them better than your competitors.

Make sure that you've added the most important details only. Include a summary too if it's possible so that your readers can quickly skim through it to get an idea about the market and won't have to spend time reading difficult text.

Management Plan

The management plan section in the business plan describes the structure of your organization and the roles of all the members of your management team. It not only states the name and responsibility of each member but also how their expertise will contribute to the overall success of the company.

One way to write the management plan section would be to divide it into the following four sections:

Ownership structure

This section should describe the legal structure of your business. It explains who owns what percentage of your company.

Internal Management Team

The internal management team should explain the main business management categories of your business. It should also include the profile of all the members that are responsible for each category.

External Management Resources

External management resources can be included in the business plan to show that you have an additional pool of expertise in case your internal management team fails to fulfill its roles. There are two sources that can be described here: Professional services and Advisory Board.

In the Professional Services section, mention all the external professional advisors like accountants, lawyers, IT consultants, etc. that your business can contact in search of guidance.

In the Advisory Board section, mention everyone who's a member of your advisory board, their titles, and their skills, and how they'll help your business become profitable. Even if you don't have an advisory board, you should still add this section in your business plan and explain how you'll set it up and who you'll approach to serve as a member on your Board.

Human Resources Needs

Explicitly describe your human resources needs here and explain the different procedures your company will go through when you're recruiting new employees. Also, include a description of the skills you're looking for in potential employees. Try to add as many specifics about staff training as possible to show how you'll get new employees ready for your company.

Operations Plan

This section needs to include information about the physical necessities of your business such as the location, equipment, and other facilities. It should also specify your inventory requirements and details about your suppliers and the manufacturing process if they're applicable to your business.

It's basically an outline of all the working capital needed by your business to run day-to-day operations. Explain to the reader how you've managed to get your business up and running, and how your products/services will be manufactured or delivered.

This will not only give the readers an insight into your business processes but also give you a list of items you need to run your business smoothly.

Critical Risks

When you did the market research for your business, you must have identified potential risk factors and problems in the industry that directly affect your business. The critical risks section of the business plan is where you can enumerate all of them so that any potential investors can learn about them and understand the necessary procedures your business has to go through to become successful.

This way, they'll be more easily convinced of the viability of your business and will be more likely to invest. Listing all the risks that your business has to undertake will also shine a light on the expertise of your management staff and further increase your credibility. Withholding important information can work against you when you're looking for new investors.

These risks involve everything you'll have to encounter during the development and growth phases of your business. They can be about the industry, or specific to your company, or even risks associated with your employees. You can also include industry trends that can significantly affect your company's performance.

Financial Projections

This is where you'll need to include your predictions about your company's financial performance in the years to come. Include numbers and statistics to get your potential investors to take your business seriously because this is an area they'll be most concerned about. Stick to the generally accepted accounting principles (GAAP) created by the Financial Accounting Standards Board(What Is GAAP? - Accounting.com, 2021). Get an accountant to review your projections to make sure they're realistic.

This section should include the following:
- Sales forecast
- Expenses budget
- Cash flow statement
- Balance sheet
- Profit and loss statement

Sales Forecast

Your sales forecast needs to show your monthly sales including the units sold, their price points, and how many of them you expect to sell, at least for the first year. For the second year and beyond, you can break them down into quarterly sales. They should be backed up with a strong understanding of the market and industry trends.

Expenses Budget

Expenses include everything from fixed costs like the money needed for insurance, rent, and other overhead costs to variable costs that can change every month like sales and advertising costs.

Cash Flow Statement

This statement shows how much cash is spent on your business monthly and how much is coming in. You can estimate this by studying your expenses budget and your sales forecasts.

Balance Sheet

Balance is the difference between the value of everything your business owns and the value of everything your business owes. The balance sheet should include all your assets and liabilities. These items can go beyond monthly expenses as well.

Profit and Loss Statement

This is where you take your sales forecasts, cash flow statement and expenses budget into consideration and predict how much your company can expect in profits or losses in the three years that are a part of your business plan.

Appendix

It's not necessary to have an appendix in your business plan, but it can be very useful. It contains all the supporting documents and information that supports or clarifies all the claims that have been made in the plan. They're added at the end because placing them between the content they support can distract readers from the point you're trying to make, which is the last thing you want to do if you're seeking potential investors for your business.

Bottom Line

It has been established that having a business plan and a business model is crucial for any new business because they provide a clear vision and a framework to follow to achieve all your targets. Furthermore, it is essential to have a solid understanding of how to generate a stable stream of revenue for your business. The Revenue Business Model enables you to fully understand the most effective techniques for generating income that not only covers your manufacturing and administrative expenses but also allows you to make a profit.

Not preparing these documents can cost you a lot down the line. You can run out of cash before you've even launched your business because you didn't anticipate the startup capital your business needed to function.

By understanding your customers and devising effective marketing strategies, you can not only retain them but also build long-lasting relationships. A clearly defined mission for your company will help you stay on track and make a meaningful impact. And with a detailed plan for revenue generation, you can turn your business into a thriving venture that makes a difference.

Get help from a business consultant if you can to prepare the perfect business plan and business model for your company.

Chapter 10

Embracing Failure

When you're starting a business, there's one thing you need to remember: Mistakes are inevitable. Even if you do everything right –hire the best team, formulate a financial plan, create effective marketing strategies, you can still make mistakes and fail from time to time. What makes failure worse is if you don't learn anything from it. It can be a blessing in disguise if you look at it with an open mind.

It's necessary to take calculated risks and plan everything before executing, but mistakes can sometimes teach you a lesson that you wouldn't have learned if you hadn't failed. They allow you to get some perspective, shine a light on your weaknesses and make you stronger as a result.

Small businesses can fail for several reasons. Lack of capital, overestimating market demand, improper management, failing to understand the customers are just a few common causes of failure. But it's important to note that this should not define you. The only way failure can hold you back from starting over is if you let it derail your hopes and stop trying.

A great way of rephrasing your situation would be to think that if everything you were doing worked out for your business then that probably means you didn't take enough risks. The fewer risks you take, the lesser you grow and learn. Staying within what's safe is truly what sets your business up for failure.

But sometimes, failure can keep you from making bigger mistakes down the line. It can make you reconsider your choices and force you to take a different route while you still can. Maybe starting a business about travel wear isn't meant for you, and when you fail in the first few months, you still have time to consider your options and figure out your next move.

While it's easier said than done, embracing and then celebrating failure is important because it gives you a chance to go over what went wrong and how you can emerge from it better than ever. Get your team in the same room and fill everyone in on the details so that everyone's on the same page. Discuss all possible solutions and ask them for their input because sometimes a small thing that escaped your mind can prove to be useful.

Types of Failure

Sometimes failing at the right time can be just what it takes for your business to become successful. If you think that failure means you need to put an end to your dreams, then you couldn't be more wrong. So many people became successful after they encountered a huge career failure. Oprah Winfrey who was fired from her first job in television is a case in point.

But before you can assess your failure and use it to your advantage, you need to understand what kind of failure it is and then make your judgment. This will make it simpler for you to figure out how you can overcome it and get back in the game.

Avoidable Failure

Avoidable failure is the kind of failure that could've been prevented but wasn't due to a lack of foresight. It happens when you don't follow the best business practices, hire the wrong people for your team, or miss crucial details during execution. It's important to learn from this failure because these mistakes can easily be avoided and shouldn't be made again as they can cost you a lot in terms of money and resources.

It allows you to analyze your company's weaknesses and make smarter decisions in the future by working on your strengths and setting practical and achievable goals for your business.

Unavoidable Failure

Unavoidable failure occurs in complex circumstances and is typically unforeseen. Because the unexpected is not in your control, you can't do anything but face the aftermath. The only way you can maybe lessen the effect is by going over all possible scenarios and taking precautionary measures just in case.

This type of failure makes you realize the need to prepare for the worst and always have a plan in place in case things go south. It can also be caused by factors beyond human control like natural disasters and accidents.

Smart Failure

Smart failure is the best of the bunch. They happen in the early stages and don't involve many resources so any loss incurred can be handled easily. Since they're smart, they provide valuable information to you about your business at the lowest cost.

It usually happens when you're trying out the trial-and-error approach, where you test out your hypotheses to see if they'll work for your business or not. It also has the simplest, most clear-cut lesson of all: If it's a success, incorporate it in your business processes, and if it's not, scrap it and rethink your strategy.

Recovering From Failure

The first thing you need to do after failing is figure out the causes behind it so you can work on the solution right away. Don't waste time ruminating on it as that will hold you back and might make things worse.

If your business fails against a competitor, you need to think logically and determine what went wrong. Maybe you need to look for a different market segment or improve your products and services, but regardless of what you have to do, you need to act fast to save yourself from a greater loss.

It's easy to start shifting the blame onto someone else and refuse to take any responsibility, but that's probably the worst thing you can do immediately after failure as it can create internal conflicts. This is a chance for you to get closer and be smarter about what to do next. If you start lashing out, you may sabotage whatever little chances you may have of minimizing the losses. You need to have a culture of openness in your organization where everyone can offer their constructive criticism and not get shot down by the people in charge.

It's also important to ask people who can look at your situation objectively and offer their advice. Since they don't have a stake in the failure, they'll have an open mind and can do a better job of pinpointing the causes and suggesting ways to overcome the failure. Sometimes, failure also brings certain people who have been holding your company back to your attention. You need to accept that you may have to let some people go to let your business truly reach its potential.

Take what you've learned and make sure you're not making the same mistakes again. Set up monitors like more frequent cash flow reporting and performance appraisals so that you're able to avoid the same failure in the future.

Getting Back on Track

Letting failure define you as an entrepreneur will not help you in any way. It's important to be emotionally strong and not take your failures personally. Letting them affect your mental health will do more damage than repair. It's not always your business practices that are at fault. Sometimes the market is simply not ready to change for your big idea and that doesn't mean it has no value.

Instead of beating yourself up over your mistakes, you need to shift your focus on the solution. You need to start thinking of ways to get back on track and make changes to your business where necessary. Don't miss your chance of recovery by focusing on the negatives. Face the music and identify ways you can do better next time.

Since you're the owner, how you respond to tragedy is crucial because your employees will look to you for answers. Seeing you in a terrible state may create ripple effects that can worsen the situation. You need to encourage them to correct their mistakes and guide them through this complicated situation.

Focus on Financial Management

To ensure your survival, you must devise a plan to manage your financial expenses and prevent the situation from getting out of hand. You must take measures to control the damage and gradually recover everything by accepting projects that you would not have previously considered. Keep a close eye on cash flow and, if possible, obtain a small loan to support your business until you can come up with an effective plan of action.

Get in Touch With Your Customers

When your customers feel the after-effects of your business failure as well, you need to make all kinds of efforts to get in touch with them and let them know about your attempts to repair the damages. If you don't act quickly and keep them updated, you might lose a huge portion of your clientele.

You also need to make sure all the services and products that have been paid for by your customers are processed to them at the earliest. Hire more workers or work extra hours to deliver every pending project as soon as possible to keep things from spiraling way beyond your control.

Reach out to Advisors and Fellow Businessmen

You shouldn't underestimate professional advisors and their level of expertise. They've seen many businesses fail and their experience has taught them a great deal about several different ways to recover from failure. You need to draw from their pool of experiences and knowledge to get back on the fast track to success.

Running a business alone can become very scary because even as an entrepreneur, you don't always have what it takes to put a team together or get through problems efficiently. You need to be encouraged and guided just like everyone else. Business mentors and advisors will provide valuable and constructive feedback and recommend the right people to you to get you started on the right foot.

You can always turn to your fellow businessmen for guidance and help because they're in the same industry and chances are that they have been in a similar situation and know of tried and tested ways to overcome it. They'll tell you about the resources you may need to utilize to get your company back to its original state and the factors you need to avoid in the future.

Reassess Your Business Goals

Setting unrealistic and unattainable standards for your business is a recipe for disaster. It's important to set measurable goals for your business so that you can take calculated steps to reach them.

When you're faced with your first-ever business failure, it's easy to feel like you've let everyone down, but sometimes failure serves as a much-needed warning that you need to take into serious consideration to avoid running into a huge loss down the road. It pushes you to go back to the drawing board, rethink your business strategies, and layout your business and financial plans to spot where you may have made a misjudgment.

Bottom Line

You only fail when you admit defeat and let failure dictate your decisions. In the business world, failure is more common than you'd think. People don't bring it up often because they refuse to let it define who they are as a business.

It opens the door to new opportunities for you as an entrepreneur or it reminds you to take measured risks in the future. It almost always serves a purpose if you're open-minded and willing to see it.

When you're starting your own company, it's important to understand yourself first. When you know your strengths, weaknesses, and profitable skills, you'll outsource and get professional help where necessary. Only people who are self-aware can achieve all they're capable of.

The road to becoming successful as an entrepreneur is full of challenges and one failure after the other. It's only your outlook and quick thinking that can get you through the roughest seas and land you safely back on your feet.

"No one said it would be easy but it sure is worth it." ~Nichcol Collins

Works Cited

(n.d.). Retrieved from MIT Education: https://web.mit.edu/22.51/www/Extras/color_theory/color.html

Articles - Investopedia . (2021, September 18). Retrieved from Investopedia: https://www.investopedia.com/articles/pf/12/small-business-challenges.asp

Blog.Hubspot. (2020, November 10). Retrieved from Hubspot: https://blog.hubspot.com/sales/data-in-sales

Business Essentials - Investopedia. (2021, April 12). Retrieved from Investopedia: https://www.investopedia.com/terms/p/patent.asp#:~:text=Utility%20patents%20are%20the%20most,years%2C%20depending%20on%20when%20filed.

Cartwright, B. (2021, June 22). *Blog.Hubspot*. Retrieved from Hubspot: https://blog.hubspot.com/marketing/color-theory-design

Copyright.gov. (n.d.). Retrieved from https://www.copyright.gov/help/faq/faq-duration.html

Hosch, W. L. (2020, May 11). *Britannica* . Retrieved from https://www.britannica.com/topic/Google-Inc/additional-info#history

Insurance Glossary - Insureon. (n.d.). Retrieved from Insureon: https://www.insureon.com/insurance-glossary/employment-practices-liability

Jones, K. (2021, March 24). *The Importance Of Branding In Business - Forbes* . Retrieved from Forbes : https://www.forbes.com/sites/forbesagencycouncil/2021/03/24/the-importance-of-branding-in-business/

Laws & Regulations - Investopedia. (2020, May 08). Retrieved from Investopedia: https://www.investopedia.com/terms/u/uniform-partnership-act-upa.asp#:~:text=Key%20Takeaways-,The%20Uniform%20Partnership%20Act%20(UPA)%20provides%20governance%20for%20business,partnerships%20in%20certain%20U.S.%20states.&text=UPA%20applies%20only%20to%20

Prakash, P. (2020, October 22). *Small Business - Nerd Wallet*. Retrieved from Nerd Wallet: https://www.nerdwallet.com/article/small-business/benefits-of-getting-an-ein

Rai, S. (2019, January 02). *6 Reasons Why Website Analytics Are Important for Your Business Growth*. Retrieved from Monster Insights : https://www.monsterinsights.com/reasons-why-website-analytics-is-important-for-your-business-growth/

Resources - Corporate Finance Institute. (n.d.). Retrieved from Corporate Finance Institute: https://corporatefinanceinstitute.com/resources/knowledge/strategy/c-corp-vs-s-corp/

The Top 12 Reasons Startups Fail - CB Insights . (2021, August 03). Retrieved from CB Insights: https://www.cbinsights.com/research/startup-failure-reasons-top/

Voigt, K., & Benson, A. (2021, April 04). *Article - Nerd Wallet*. Retrieved from Nerd Wallet : https://www.nerdwallet.com/article/investing/what-is-a-financial-plan

What Is GAAP? - Accounting.com. (2021, September 07). Retrieved from Accounting.com: https://www.accounting.com/resources/gaap/#:~:text=Generally%20accepted%20accounting%20principles%2C%20or,approved%20accounting%20methods%20and%20practices.

Wheeler, K. (2021, January 2019). *Blog.Hubspot*. Retrieved from Hubspot: https://blog.hubspot.com/agency/develop-brand-identity

Printed in the USA
CPSIA information can be obtained
at www.ICGtesting.com
CBHW041829111124
17254CB00016BA/185

9 781662 899928